WordPress®
on**Demand**

Patrice-Anne Rutledge

QUE® Que Publishing, 800 East 96th Street, Indianapolis, IN 46240 USA

WordPress® on Demand

ISBN-13: 978-0-7897-5037-2
ISBN-10: 0-7897-5037-6

Library of Congress Control Number: 2013935191

Printed in the United States of America

First Printing: May 2013

Bulk Sales

Que Publishing offers excellent discounts on this book when ordered in quantity for bulk purchases or special sales. For more information, please contact

U.S. Corporate and Government Sales
1-800-382-3419
corpsales@pearsontechgroup.com

For sales outside of the U.S., please contact

International Sales
international@pearson.com

Editor-in-Chief
Greg Wiegand

Acquisitions Editor
Michelle Newcomb

Development Editor
Charlotte Kughen

Managing Editor
Kristy Hart

Project Editor
Andy Beaster

Copy Editor
Barbara Hacha

Indexer
Lisa Stumpf

Proofreader
Dan Knott

Technical Editor
Morten Rand-Hendriksen

Publishing Coordinator
Cindy Teeters

Cover Designer
Anne Jones

Compositor
Bumpy Design

Dedication

To my family, with thanks for their ongoing support and encouragement.

Acknowledgments

Special thanks to Michelle Newcomb, Charlotte Kughen, Andy Beaster, Barbara Hacha, Betsy Gratner, and Morten Rand-Hendriksen for their feedback, suggestions, and attention to detail.

a

About the Author

Patrice-Anne Rutledge is a business technology author, journalist, and long-time WordPress user who specializes in teaching others to maximize the power of new technologies. She is also the author of numerous other books for Pearson Education, including *Sams Teach Yourself LinkedIn in 10 Minutes, Sams Teach Yourself Google+ in 10 Minutes, Using Facebook, The Truth About Profiting from Social Networking,* and *PowerPoint 2013 Absolute Beginner's Guide.* You can reach Patrice through her website at www.patricerutledge.com.

We Want to Hear from You!

As the reader of this book, *you* are our most important critic and commentator. We value your opinion and want to know what we're doing right, what we could do better, what areas you'd like to see us publish in, and any other words of wisdom you're willing to pass our way.

As an associate publisher for Que Publishing, I welcome your comments. You can email or write me directly to let me know what you did or didn't like about this book—as well as what we can do to make our books better.

Please note that I cannot help you with technical problems related to the topic of this book. We do have a User Services group, however, where I will forward specific technical questions related to the book.

When you write, please be sure to include this book's title and author as well as your name, email address, and phone number. I will carefully review your comments and share them with the author and editors who worked on the book.

Email: feedback@quepublishing.com

Mail: Greg Wiegand
         Editor-in-Chief
         Que Publishing
         800 East 96th Street
         Indianapolis, IN 46240 USA

Reader Services

Visit our website and register this book at quepublishing.com/register for convenient access to any updates, downloads, or errata that might be available for this book.

Contents

C

Introduction

What You'll Learn

Welcome to *WordPress on Demand*, a visual guide to one of the world's most popular web design applications. By choosing WordPress, you have plenty of company: millions of people—from individual bloggers to large organizations—have used WordPress to create websites.

This book is based on WordPress version 3.5.1. If you're using an earlier version of WordPress, you should update. If you're using a later version of WordPress, you might notice a few feature changes, but the basic functionality of Word-Press will remain the same.

WordPress on Demand is designed to get you up and running on WordPress as quickly as possible. Because knowing how to use WordPress features is just part of creating a successful website, *WordPress on Demand* also provides tips on website best practices in each chapter. For now, turn to Chapter 1, "Introducing WordPress," to get started with this powerful, yet easy-to-use web design tool.

Who This Book Is For

This book is for you if...

- ◆ You want to become productive with WordPress as quickly as possible and are short on time.

- ◆ You're new to WordPress—and designing websites—and need to learn the basics in an easy-to-understand format.

- ◆ You're a visual learner and want illustrated, step-by-step guidance on learning WordPress.

How You'll Learn

What You'll Learn

Who This Book Is For

Step-by-Step Instructions

Organization of the Book

Step-by-Step Instructions

This book provides concise step-by-step instructions that show you how to accomplish a task. Each set of instructions includes illustrations that directly correspond to the easy-to-follow steps. Also included in the text are timesavers, tables, checklists, and sidebars to help you work more efficiently or to teach you more in-depth information. A "Did You Know?" feature provides tips and techniques to help you work smarter, and a "See Also" feature directs you to other parts of the book containing related information about the task.

Workshops

Throughout *WordPress on Demand*, you learn the basic techniques required to create a quality WordPress website. With the Workshops, you move beyond the basics and try some real-world WordPress projects. The Workshops file is available on the web at www.queondemand.com. To access the online Workshops file, follow these simple steps:

1. Go to queondemand.com/register and sign in or create an account.

2. To register this product to your account, enter 9780789750372 into the box, and click Submit.

3. Answer challenge question to show proof of purchase.

4. On the Registered Products area of your account page, you will now see an "Access Bonus Content" link—click that link to be taken to the page with the bonus material for this title.

5. You may return to the bonus material at any time by clicking on this link, which appears in your account. (Must be logged in to view.)

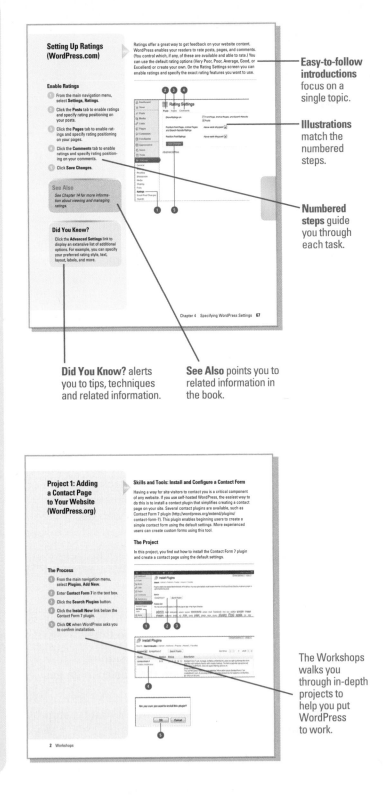

Easy-to-follow introductions focus on a single topic.

Illustrations match the numbered steps.

Numbered steps guide you through each task.

Did You Know? alerts you to tips, techniques and related information.

See Also points you to related information in the book.

The Workshops walks you through in-depth projects to help you put WordPress to work.

Organization of the Book

WordPress on Demand is organized into chapters based on common WordPress tasks in the order you'll most likely encounter them. To distinguish between the two versions of WordPress, chapters and sections are labeled with **WordPress.com** to identify features specific to hosted WordPress and **WordPress.org** to identify features specific to self-hosted WordPress.

Chapter 1, "Introducing WordPress"—The first chapter of this book introduces you to WordPress, a free software application that enables you to quickly create a quality website. You also learn to choose between the two versions of WordPress: hosted WordPress.com and self-hosted WordPress. If you're new to WordPress, this chapter also gives you a quick overview of WordPress basics, web hosting, domain names, and website planning.

Chapter 2, "Getting Started with WordPress.com"—WordPress.com enables you to create a website without having to install any software or worry about backups, configuration, or plugins. If you decide that hosted WordPress.com is the right WordPress solution for you, this chapter shows you how to get up and running as quickly as possible.

Chapter 3, "Getting Started with WordPress.org"—Using self-hosted WordPress gives you complete control over your website, including the capability to use custom themes, install plugins, implement e-commerce functionality, and modify code. If you decide self-hosted WordPress is the right solution for you, this chapter shows you how to install WordPress and set up your site.

Chapter 4, "Specifying WordPress Settings"—By customizing your WordPress settings, often a one-time task, you can better manage your site, receive only the notifications you want, and avoid any unpleasant surprises. In this chapter, you discover how to customize your site structure, comments, sharing options, privacy, and more.

Chapter 5, "Working with Themes"—A theme defines the structure and appearance of your website. A theme isn't a single file, but rather a collection of files including a stylesheet, image files, and templates. In this chapter, you find out how to select, upload, and activate themes, as well as how to customize their appearance to suit your needs.

Chapter 6, "Creating and Managing Pages"—Pages are an important part of your WordPress site, enabling you to create static content that's not part of your blog or feed. In this chapter, you find out how to create, manage, and delete pages. If you use WordPress.com, you can also save time by copying existing pages.

Chapter 7, "Creating and Managing Posts"—Posts are the foundation of any blog, or the blog portion of a website. Your posts are also included in your site's feed, which readers can subscribe to. In Chapter 7, you discover the many ways to create a post in WordPress, how to manage and edit existing posts, and how to apply categories and tags to your posts.

Chapter 8, "Formatting Pages and Posts"—WordPress makes it easy to precisely format the content you enter on your website's pages and posts. In addition to traditional formatting options, such as adding bold and italic to text, creating lists, inserting links, and checking spelling, WordPress also offers several advanced formatting features. In this chapter, you're introduced to basic formatting techniques using both the Visual Editor and the Text Editor.

Chapter 9, "Working with Media Files"—One of the best ways to enliven your WordPress site is with media files, including images, audio, video, and other documents. This chapter shows you how to upload files from your computer, insert them from a URL, create eye-catching image galleries, and embed media from sites such as YouTube, Vimeo, SlideShare, and Twitter.

Chapter 10, "Working with Widgets"—WordPress widgets enable you to add content to your website sidebars. For example, you can use widgets to display information about yourself or your business, contact details, blog categories, your latest posts, links or buttons to your site feed or external sites, your latest Twitter tweets, a Facebook Like box, images, advertising, and much more. In this chapter, you discover that with a little imagination, you can display almost anything you want in your sidebars.

Chapter 11, "Working with Links"—WordPress gives you the option to display links on your sidebar, including both internal and external links. For example, you could create a blogroll of your favorite websites or link to your published articles on other sites, your current clients or projects, or even specific pages or posts on your own site. Learn how to make the most of this optional feature, including working with link categories.

Chapter 12, "Working with Plugins (WordPress.org)"— Plugins enable you to extend the power of self-hosted WordPress with additional functionality. The benefit of using plugins is that you can select only the functionality you need without overloading your WordPress site with unnecessary features. For example, you can install and activate plugins to perform automated site backups, control spam, sell products and services, embed audio and video, display content sliders, create a membership site, enhance your site's SEO, connect with social sites such as Facebook or Twitter, and much more.

Chapter 13, "Adding and Managing Menus"—Your website's menu is an important navigational tool, but a properly structured menu can do much more than direct visitors to the content on your site. The right menu can also help retain visitors and encourage sales. In this chapter, you find out how to change page menu order and labels and create custom menus.

Chapter 14, "Getting Feedback on Your Website (WordPress.com)"—Receiving feedback on your website, before and after publication, is an important part of its success. WordPress.com offers several built-in tools that gather feedback from both internal and external audiences. You can receive post and page feedback from your colleagues before you publish, add polls to survey your readers about a specific topic, enable ratings on individuals posts and pages, and publish a contact form to encourage readers to contact you.

Chapter 15, "Using WordPress.com Premium Features"—WordPress.com offers several premium features that you can purchase. These upgrades enable you to upload audio and video to your site, register and map to a custom domain name, remove ads, increase storage space, and more.

Chapter 16, "Managing Users"—Working on your WordPress website doesn't have to be a solo project. WordPress offers several user roles that give other people varying levels of access: everything from complete control of your site to the capability to create posts without actually publishing them.

Chapter 17, "Managing Comments"—Reader interaction is one of the most important components of a successful blog. Fortunately, WordPress makes it easy to develop a community on your site with its powerful commenting tools. By default, WordPress installs Akismet, a powerful spam-management tool, when you create your website. If you use self-hosted WordPress, you also have the option of installing a third-party commenting plugin with even more powerful community-building features.

Chapter 18, "Managing Your WordPress Website"— In this chapter, you learn to handle all the important "behind the scenes" tasks involved in managing a successful website, including managing backups, security, updates, imports, exports, and more. Fortunately, WordPress offers tools that simplify all these tasks.

Appendix A, "WordPress Premium Themes"—
Purchasing a WordPress premium theme can be a good
option for users who want advanced features, professional design, support, and updates. In this appendix,
you explore several good options for premium themes.

Appendix B, "WordPress Plugins (WordPress.org)"—
Plugins can take your self-hosted WordPress website
from ordinary to extraordinary with a variety of content
enhancements. Behind the scenes, plugins can simplify,
streamline, and secure the process of managing your
site. In this appendix, you explore some of the most
popular WordPress plugins.

Appendix C, "Going Mobile with WordPress,"—
WordPress makes it easy to update your site on the go
with mobile apps designed for many popular smartphones and tablets. Although these apps don't enable
you to access every WordPress feature, you can post,
upload photos, and manage comments wherever you
are. In addition, this appendix also introduces you to
several mobile plugins that make it easy for your readers to view your site on their own mobile devices.

Introducing WordPress

WordPress is a free software application that enables you to quickly create a quality website. The flexibility WordPress offers makes it a suitable tool for everyone from a casual user with limited technical skills to an experienced developer looking to create a sophisticated, custom website.

If you're new to WordPress—or to creating websites—this chapter gives you a quick overview of WordPress, web hosting, domain names, and website planning.

Understanding the Difference Between WordPress.com and WordPress.org

WordPress offers two versions:

◆ **WordPress.com**—Hosted, web-based software. With this option, you create your website at wordpress.com without any worries about installation, upgrades, backups, or security. This solution is ideal for people who want to avoid the technical aspects of creating a website. The trade-off is less flexibility and control over design and features.

WordPress.com URL

WordPress.com website

Follow WordPress.com sites you enjoy

Menu offers easy navigation

Blog posts display chronological content

Feeds to subscribe to your posts and comments

Built-in sidebar options

◆ **WordPress.org**—Self-hosted software you install and set up yourself through a web host. Although you can download this version of WordPress at wordpress.org, most web hosts offer an automated installation tool. This solution is ideal for tech-savvy people who want complete control over their websites, including the capability to use custom themes, install plugins, implement e-commerce functionality, and modify code.

IMPORTANT *Although both versions of WordPress are similar, distinct differences exist as well. Because this book covers both, sections specific to WordPress.com are labeled* **WordPress.com** *and sections specific to self-hosted WordPress are labeled* **WordPress.org**. *Everything else pertains to both hosted and self-hosted WordPress.*

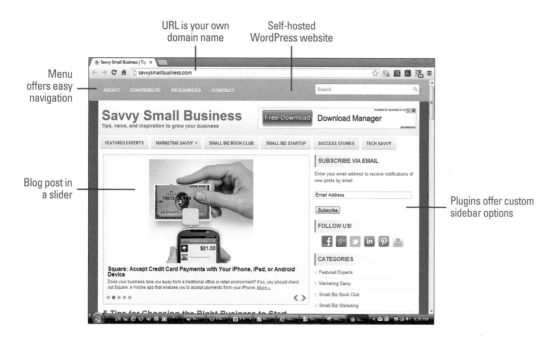

URL is your own domain name

Self-hosted WordPress website

Menu offers easy navigation

Blog post in a slider

Plugins offer custom sidebar options

Exploring WordPress Versions

The following table provides more details about the distinct differences between hosted and self-hosted WordPress.

Did You Know?

Looking for a completely free website? WordPress.com without any upgrades is the option for you. Although this choice still provides many powerful features, you should at least consider purchasing your own domain name (starting at $18 per year) if you want to create a professional presence on the Web.

WordPress.com Versus WordPress.org Features

Feature	WordPress.com	WordPress.org
Hosting and setup	Included.	Web host required to install and set up WordPress (self-hosted).
Upgrades	Included.	Manual upgrades to WordPress, themes, and plugins.
Backups and security	Included.	Install a plugin to manage your own backups and security.
Themes	More than 200 free and premium themes available. Upload of custom themes not allowed.	Upload any theme you choose, including custom themes.
Plugins	No plugins. You must use the features and tools WordPress.com provides.	Thousands of plugins to choose from, offering numerous features and enhancements.
Domain name	Optional. Can use free hosted domain name (yoursite.wordpress.com) or purchase your own domain name.	Purchase your own domain name.
Advertisements (such as AdSense, affiliate product ads, or your own ads)	Not allowed.	Allowed.
E-commerce/shopping cart	Not available. Only option is to place a PayPal button on a page or sidebar.	Numerous e-commerce and shopping cart plugins are available, both free and fee-based.
PHP code modification	Not allowed.	Allowed.

Website Versus Blog: What's the Difference?

One common area of confusion for new users is the difference between a website and a blog.

A *website* is essentially any site available on the Web. A *blog* is a type of website—or section of a website—that displays dated posts in chronological order. Although WordPress is commonly associated with blogging, you can use it to create a website with or without a blog component.

In this book, I use website generically (often shortened to site) to refer to any kind of website or blog you can create using WordPress.

Understanding Web Hosting

If you plan to use self-hosted WordPress, you need to select a web host to make your site accessible on the Web.

> **IMPORTANT** *If you plan to use WordPress.com, you don't need to select a web host. WordPress.com is a hosted solution, and web hosting is included.*

The minimum technical requirements for a web host to run WordPress include

◆ PHP version 5.2.4 or later

◆ MySQL version 5.0 or later

Don't worry if you aren't familiar with PHP or MySQL. You don't need knowledge of these to create a successful site. Just be sure to select a web host that meets these requirements.

The following web hosts offer automated WordPress installation and are good choices for WordPress websites:

◆ Bluehost (www.bluehost.com)

◆ Dreamhost (www.dreamhost.com)

◆ HostGator (www.hostgator.com)

Most web hosts offer multiple plans. When choosing a plan, consider price, but also consider the number of domains you require, whether you need unlimited storage and data transfer, and so forth. If you're just creating a single website with modest traffic demands, a basic hosting account should be sufficient. If you plan to create multiple websites, or anticipate heavy traffic, compare features carefully before selecting a plan.

Understanding Domain Names

A domain name refers to the URL or web address people use to reach your website, such as http://www.quepublishing.com.

WordPress.com offers two options for domain names. You can use the free, default address that comes with your WordPress.com account, such as http://globetrottingchef.wordpress.com. Or you can map your account to a unique domain name you purchase, such as http://www.globetrottingchef.com.

Self-hosted WordPress requires a unique domain name so that you can install WordPress on your own website. You can purchase a domain name at the time you sign up for a web hosting account or use a domain name you previously purchased.

Your domain registrar and web host don't have to be the same company, but it's often simpler if they are. For example, if you purchased a domain name from GoDaddy several months ago and now decide you want to host your website with HostGator, you can do so.

IMPORTANT *Think carefully before choosing your domain name. Although you can change this name, it's best to avoid the hassle and expense of doing so. Your choice of domain name is particularly important for a business website.*

Planning Your Website

The key to a successful website is a solid plan. Here's a simple six-step process for planning your new site.

TIMESAVER *Although you're probably eager to get started on your website, you should take some time to create a solid plan first. Doing so avoids costly and time-consuming rework.*

IMPORTANT *One of the biggest challenges first-time web designers face is being too ambitious. If you're creating a basic website for a new business, for example, you don't need hundreds of pages and sophisticated features to launch. Start with the basics and build from there, in phases.*

Step 1—Determine Your Website Goals

First, clearly articulate the focus and goals of your website. Here are several questions to ask:

◆ What do I want to achieve with this website? Do I want to sell products or services, share my expertise with the world, or spread the word about a special cause?

- What content or structure will help me achieve my goals?

- Who is my target audience? What are they looking for?

- What keywords are most relevant to the focus of my website? Good key-words include the types of products and services you offer, the topics you cover on your blog, and so forth. Your business name is a good keyword only if people know your name and might search for it.

- What are my competitors doing and how can I make my site better?

Step 2—Select a WordPress Version

Decide whether you want to use hosted WordPress.com or self-hosted WordPress. This decision has an effect on the features available to you and, as a result, on your overall website plan.

See "Understanding the Difference Between WordPress.com and WordPress.org" earlier in this chapter for more information.

Step 3—Choose a Domain Name

The right domain name can make a big difference in how your website is per-ceived and the audience it attracts.

See "Understanding Domain Names" earlier in this chapter for more informa-tion about WordPress domain options and choosing the best name for your site.

Step 4—Develop a Structure for Your Website

Before creating your website, you need to have a good idea about its content and structure. At a minimum, you should map out your pages, subpages, blog catego-ries, menu structure, and sidebar structure.

TIMESAVER *Not sure how to best organize your website or what pages you might need? Do a little competitor intelligence. Look at other sites in your niche for inspiration and ideas, both for what you want—and don't want—on your own site. Looking at popular sites you admire outside of your niche can also provide inspiration.*

Posts Versus Pages

A common question WordPress beginners have is determining the difference between a post and a page. Although pages and posts are covered in detail in later chapters, here's a quick definition for your planning purposes.

Posts are the foundation of any blog—or the blog portion of a website. Although creating a post is very similar to creating a page, posts perform a different function on your site. On most sites, posts display on your home page (in chronological order, newest post first) or on a dedicated blog page. Your posts are also included in your site's feed, which readers can subscribe to.

A page enables you to create static content that's not part of your blog or feed. For example, pages for a business site might include About Us, Meet the Team, Clients, Products, Services, and Contact Us. (You can probably get more creative with the names, though!) If your site is primarily a blog, you might need fewer pages, such as one about your blog and one for contacting you.

> **See Also**
>
> *See Chapter 6, "Creating and Managing Pages," and Chapter 7, "Creating and Managing Posts," for more information about WordPress pages and posts.*

Here are some questions to ask:

- ◆ What pages does my site need?
- ◆ In what order should I place these pages on my menu?
- ◆ Should I use subpages, and if so, what should they be?

Subpages on a menu

- How should I categorize my blog posts? Which categories and subcategories do I need?

- What content should I display on my sidebar?

Email subscription

Social follow buttons

Sample WordPress sidebar

Did You Know?

When considering content for your sidebar, focus on the actions you want your readers to take rather than loading it with as much content as possible. For example, you might want to include a newsletter signup form, a link to your blog feed, or social sharing buttons (for Facebook, Twitter, and so forth).

See Also

See Chapter 10, "Working with Widgets," for more information about working with sidebars.

TIMESAVER *Creating an editorial calendar for your blog posts can save time and make it easier to post consistently. When getting started, create a calendar for your first month's posts. You can always revise your calendar as needed to accommodate reader feedback or breaking news.*

Step 5—Choose a Theme

Before you set up your WordPress website, it's a good idea to select a starting theme. This helps you visualize what your site would look like when complete and also could have an effect on your content choices.

See Also

See Chapter 5, "Working with Themes," for more information about selecting and installing themes.

You can preview available themes for WordPress.com at http://theme.wordpress.com. You can preview themes for self-hosted WordPress at http://wordpress.org/extend/themes.

Step 6—Create Your Site

With your plan in place, get started on your new website! The remaining chapters in this book guide you step by step through everything you need to create a quality WordPress website.

IMPORTANT *Don't worry too much about creating the "perfect" plan for your website. WordPress is very flexible, and you can change pages, menu structure, categories, plugins, and themes as you design your site.*

Getting Started with WordPress.com

WordPress.com enables you to create a website without having to install any software or worry about backups, configuration, or plugins. If you decide that hosted WordPress.com is the right WordPress solution for you, this chapter shows you how to get up and running as quickly as possible.

Creating a Website with WordPress.com

TIMESAVER *Before creating your site, read through this section to determine which options you prefer. Then you can create your site quickly without having to stop and make decisions as you go.*

Create a Website with WordPress.com

1 Navigate to https://wordpress.com.

2 Click the **Get Started** button.

IMPORTANT *Don't worry that you're locked into the choices you make when you first sign up. Word-Press.com is flexible, giving you the option to make changes after you create your basic site, such as purchasing an upgrade, registering a domain name, changing your theme, and so forth.*

Did You Know?

Although WordPress.com uses the term "blog" to describe your site, you can create much more than a series of chronological posts with Word-Press.com; you can even create a complete business website. For more information about the differences between blogs and websites, see Chapter 1, "Introducing WordPress."

Creating a website with WordPress.com couldn't be easier. You navigate to wordpress.com and start the signup process. Although you can set up a site at no cost, WordPress.com does offer some extras worth considering, particularly if you're creating a web presence for a business. Here are your options:

- **Account type**—Choose between three account types: a free Basic account or a fee-based Premium or Business account (see the sidebar "WordPress.com Account Options" later in this chapter for more details).

- **Domain name**—Register your own domain name (such as yourname.com) for a fee or use the free domain WordPress.com provides (such as yourname.wordpress.com).

- **Theme**—Use a free theme or purchase a premium theme for a fee.

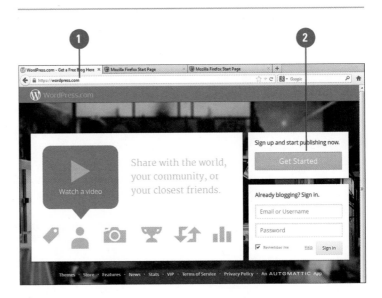

3 Enter your email address.

4 Enter a username that contains at least four characters and includes only lowercase letters and numbers.

5 Enter a password for accessing your account.

IMPORTANT *Store your password in a secure location so that you can easily log in to WordPress again.*

6 Enter your preferred blog address. By default, WordPress suggests a free address (hosted on wordpress.com), but you can also select a .me, .com, .net, or .org address for a fee.

IMPORTANT *If your chosen address isn't available, WordPress informs you of this, and you need to select another name.*

Did You Know?

You can start with a free address and upgrade to a paid domain name at a later date.

Did You Know?

To make your password more secure, use both uppercase and lowercase letters, numbers, and symbols. Optionally, click the **Generate Strong Password** button to have WordPress generate a password for you.

3

WordPress.com   Log In   Themes   Support   News   Features   Sign Up

Get started with WordPress.com by filling out this simple form:

E-mail Address ✓
sara.wretstrom1@gmail.com

We'll send you an email to activate your account, so please **triple-check** that you've typed it correctly.

Username ✓
sarawretstrom

Your username should be a minimum of four characters and can only include lowercase letters and numbers.

4

5

Password
EH7fxcbM8DK&6!Y!W8dCwpcPxy$ 👁 Hide

Great passwords use upper and lower case characters, numbers, and symbols like !"£$%^&(.

🔑 Generate strong password

Blog Address ✓
granitecovedesign   .wordpress.com Free ▼

Choose an address for your blog. You can change the WordPress.com address later.

If you don't want a blog you can signup for just a username.

Did you know, the address **granitecovedesign.com** is also available?

Great! Use this address on my blog for $18 a year   No thanks, I'll use the free address.

6

7 Click the **Sign Up** button below the account option you prefer: Basic, Premium, or Business. See the sidebar "WordPress.com Account Options" for more information about the differences among these three options. In this example, you sign up for a free account.

8 WordPress prompts you to check your email to complete the registration process and activate your account.

IMPORTANT *You have only two days to activate your account. If you don't do so during this timeframe, you need to start over and sign up again. See "Activating and Setting Up your WordPress.com Account" later in this chapter for more information about the next steps in the signup process.*

Basic		Premium		Business	
Great for basic blogging	$0 for life	Great for pro bloggers	$99 per year	Great for businesses	$199 per year
⊘ Free blog!		⊘ Free blog!		⊘ Free blog!	
⊘ WordPress.com address		⊘ A .com, .net, .org, or .me address		⊘ A .com, .net, .org, or .me address	
⊘ Basic customization		⊘ Advanced customization		⊘ Advanced customization	
* No premium themes included		* No premium themes included		★ 50+ premium themes included	
* No video storage		▪▪ Store dozens of videos		▪▪ Store Unlimited videos	
▪ 3 GB of space		▪▪ 13 GB of space		▪▪ Unlimited space	
▪ Community support		▪▪ Direct Email support		▪▪ Live Chat support	
SIGN UP		SIGN UP		SIGN UP	

7

8

WordPress.com   Log In   Themes   Support   News   Features   Sign Up

Now Check Your E-mail to Complete Registration

An e-mail has been sent to sara.wretstrom1@gmail.com to activate your account. Check your inbox and click the link in the message. It should arrive within 30 minutes. If you do not activate your account within two days, you will have to sign up again.

Didn't get your email yet?

Click to request another email

Optionally, let WordPress know more about your plans

WordPress.com Account Options

Before creating a website using WordPress.com, you should decide which type of account you want: Basic, Premium, or Business.

WordPress.com Account Types	Basic	Premium	Business
Annual Cost	Free	$99	$199
URL	[yourname].wordpress.com	Your own .com, .net, .me, or .org address	Your own .com, .net, .me, or .org address
Customization	Basic	Font and CSS editing capabilities	Font and CSS editing capabilities
Premium themes	None; must purchase premium themes for an additional fee	None; must purchase premium themes for an additional fee	All premium themes included
Video storage	None; must purchase VideoPress upgrade for an additional fee	VideoPress upgrade included	VideoPress upgrade included with unlimited storage
Space	3GB	13GB	Unlimited
Support	Community	Direct email	Live chat

Activating and Setting Up Your WordPress.com Account

After you sign up on WordPress.com, you receive an email requesting you to activate your blog. This process leads you through six setup steps. My recommendation is to skip WordPress setup steps 1, 2, 5, and 6 for now. (Note that these are WordPress.com steps, not steps in this book section.) You can complete these after you learn more about WordPress and have started working on your site.

Activate and Set Up Your WordPress.com Account

1. Click the **Activate Blog** button in the email WordPress sends you.

2. In WordPress step 1, optionally follow interesting topics and click **Next Step** to continue.

Did You Know?

On WordPress.com you can follow topics that interest you, such as art or books, and then view related blog posts in your WordPress Reader.

Did You Know?

To skip an optional step, click **Next Step** without taking an action.

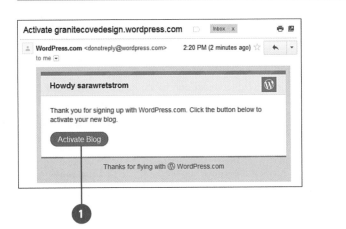

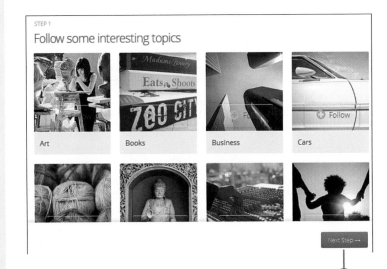

3 In WordPress step 2, optionally click the **Connect** link next to any social site you want to search for potential friends on WordPress. com. Click **Follow** to the right of the friends you want to follow, and click **Next Step** to continue. See "Finding and Following Friends" later in this chapter for more information.

4 In WordPress step 3, enter a **Blog Title**.

5 Enter a **Tagline** that describes your site. With most themes, this displays below your blog title.

6 Select a **Language** from the drop-down list if the default isn't your preferred language.

7 Click **Next Step** to continue.

STEP 2

Follow Your Friends

Are your Facebook, Twitter, and Google friends blogging with WordPress? Give the friend finder a whirl to find out.

🐦 Twitter   Connected

☐ Automatically send my posts to Twitter.

📘 Facebook   Connect

Ⓜ Google   Connect

We'll display your friends with WordPress blogs here. Try following Matt; he'll be your friend

← Back to previous step   Next Step →

STEP 3

Set up your blog

Blog Title   Granite Cove Design

Tagline (optional)   Contemporary, Eco-friendly Interior Design

In a few words, explain what your blog is about.

Language   en - English

Which language will you be blogging in?

← Back to previous step   Next Step →

8 In WordPress step 4, select a theme and click **Next Step** to continue. You can use the default Twenty Twelve theme or search for a theme that better matches your site goals.

9 In WordPress step 5, optionally click the **Customize It!** button to customize your theme design and click **Next Step** to continue.

See Also

See Chapter 5, "Working with Themes," for more information about selecting and customizing a theme.

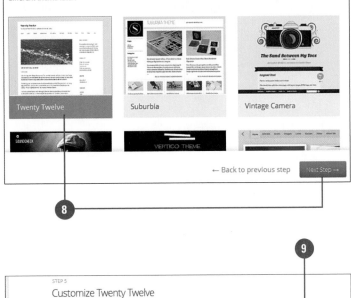

10. In WordPress step 6, optionally create your first post using text, a photo, a video, a quote, or a link and click **Finish** to complete the setup process.

11. A welcome screen displays, with options for exploring WordPress.com or starting on your new site.

Did You Know?

If you want to hide your work-in-progress website until it's ready to face the world, you can temporarily make it private. To do so, select **Settings**, **Reading** from the navigation menu, and select the **I Would Like My Site to Be Private, Visible Only to Users I Choose** option button.

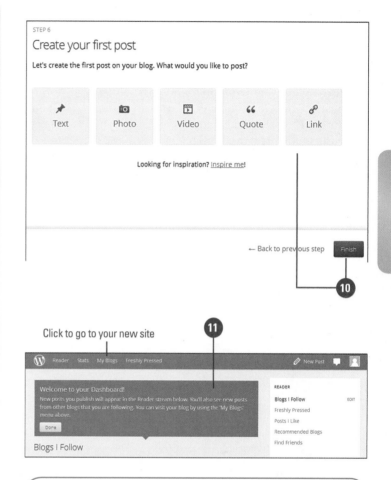

STEP 6

Create your first post

Let's create the first post on your blog. What would you like to post?

Text   Photo   Video   Quote   Link

Looking for inspiration? Inspire me!

← Back to previous step   Finish

Click to go to your new site

Welcome to your Dashboard!
New posts you publish will appear in the Reader stream below. You'll also see new posts from other blogs that you are following. You can visit your blog by using the 'My Blogs' menu above.

Done

Blogs I Follow

For Your Information

WordPress.com Themes

A *theme* controls the appearance of your site and is a framework for your own content, such as pages, posts, and media files. WordPress offers both free themes and premium themes you must purchase. Premium themes display a price in the lower-right corner of their thumbnail image.

If the themes that display on this screen don't suit you, you can search for more themes by clicking the **View More Themes** button. If you're not sure which theme to choose, just keep the default theme (Twenty Twelve) for now. You can change your theme at any time. This isn't your only chance to select the right theme.

Navigating WordPress.com

The left side of every WordPress screen includes a vertical navigation menu, divided into categories, that helps you find WordPress features. The selected category displays menu options below its heading. To view menu options for another category, pause your mouse over it. If you decide that the menu is taking up too much space, you can collapse it by clicking **Collapse Menu** at the bottom of the menu. This leaves you with only icons as your navigational tool.

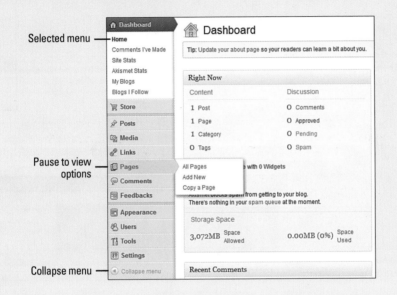

Exploring the WordPress.com Admin Bar

The Admin Bar displays at the top of the Word-Press.com screen when you're logged in. On this bar, you can do the following:

◆ Click the WordPress icon to open Reader, which displays posts from the blogs you follow in chronological order.

◆ Pause your mouse over the WordPress icon to view a shortcut menu to create a new post, view notifications and stats, view your blogs, and adjust your settings.

◆ Click your site name to view your site in a browser.

◆ Pause your mouse over your site name to view a short menu of popular WordPress features.

◆ Click your username to view a shortcut menu for finding friends, managing your blogs, getting help, or signing out.

The Admin Bar offers different options when you're viewing another WordPress.com site other than your own. In this case, the Admin Bar displays the following options when you view a post:

◆ **Follow**—Follow this site and display posts in Reader.

◆ **Like**—Show your support by liking the post.

◆ **Reblog**—Post to your own site, adding your own commentary.

TIMESAVER *If you're already following a blog, the Follow link becomes the Following link. Click this again to unfollow the blog.*

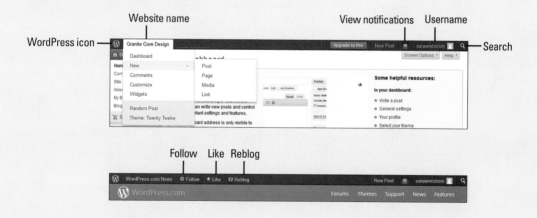

WordPress icon — Website name — View notifications — Username — Search

Follow Like Reblog

Exploring the WordPress.com Dashboard

When you log in to WordPress, you view the Dashboard. From this WordPress activity hub, you can

◆ View current information about your posts, pages, and comments in the Right Now box.

◆ Create a basic post using the QuickPress box.

◆ View your recent drafts and comments.

◆ View stats about your website activity.

◆ View WordPress.com news.

Did You Know?

You can click the **Screen Options** button to control what displays on your Dashboard. You can also drag and drop content to rearrange it.

Temporary content for a new site

Info about your site

Create a quick post

Logging In to WordPress.com

Whenever you want to work on your WordPress.com site, you can log in with your username (or email) and password.

Log In to WordPress.com

1. Navigate to your login screen, such as http://granitecovedesign. wordpress.com/wp-login.php.

    TIMESAVER *You can also log in at http://www.wordpress.com.*

2. Enter your username or email address.

3. Enter your password.

4. If you want WordPress to remember your username and password, select the **Remember Me** check box.

    IMPORTANT *If you're logging in from a public computer, you should leave the **Remember Me** box unchecked.*

5. Click the **Log In** button to log in to WordPress.

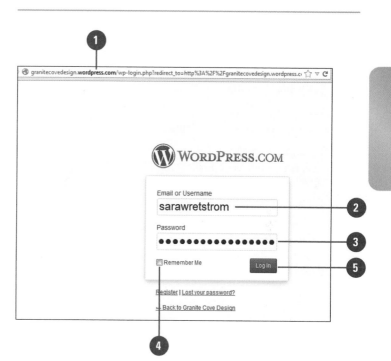

Did You Know?

If you can't remember your password, click the **Lost Your Password?** link to create a new one. You can also change your password manually on the Personal Settings screen (see the "Defining Your Personal Settings" section later in this chapter).

Creating Your WordPress.com Profile

Before you start working on your website itself, you should create your profile. WordPress.com uses your profile and related photo as a means of identification. A good profile also helps you grow your site and connect with others.

Create Your WordPress.com Profile

1 From the main navigation menu, select **Users**, **My Profile**.

2 In the Basic Details section, enter your name, location, and a brief bio.

3 Click the **Change Your Gravatar** link to add a Gravatar to your profile. For most users, this should be a flattering headshot.

IMPORTANT *Any information you enter on your profile displays publicly on your website and on your Gravatar hovercard.*

See Also

If you aren't the only person contributing content to your site, see Chapter 16, "Managing Users," to learn more about adding additional users.

Did You Know?

If you don't want to use Gravatar hovercards on your site, deselect the **Gravatar Hovercards** check box. This feature is enabled by default.

Did You Know?

In addition to WordPress, companies such as HootSuite (social media management) and Disqus (blog commenting) use Gravatar.

Gravatars and Gravatar Hovercards

A *Gravatar* is a globally recognized avatar, a small image that displays next to your name on posts and comments across the Web. You have several options for adding a Gravatar: upload an image from your computer, use your webcam to take a picture of yourself, use a link to an image stored online, or use a previous WordPress.com avatar. You can also manage your Gravatar online at http://en.gravatar.com.

A Gravatar hovercard displays when you pause your mouse over a Gravatar, such as one next to a blog post or comment. You can also preview your hovercard on the Discussion Settings screen (select **Settings**, **Discussions** from the navigation menu). Scroll down to the Avatars section and pause your mouse over your Gravatar to view it.

Gravatar next to a comment

Gravatar hovercard

④ In the Contacts section, enter any public contact information, such as a business email or phone number.

⑤ Click the **Add Photo Through Gravatar** button to upload additional photos to your profile.

⑥ In the Links section, enter any links you want to display on your profile and click the **Add Link** button. For example, you might want to display a link to your website if you're using WordPress.com specifically for a blog.

⑦ In the Verified External Services section, select a service from the drop-down list and click the **Verify Through Gravatar** button. Word-Press displays any services you verify on your profile and uses this as a means of authenticating your identity. Some external services you can add include Blogger, Facebook, Twitter, Tumblr, and LinkedIn.

⑧ Click the **Update Profile** button.

Did You Know?

In addition to WordPress, companies such as HootSuite (social media management) and Disqus (blog commenting) use Gravatar.

---

④

Contacts

Fill out any contact methods you would like to make available publicly.

Public Email

AIM

GTalk

ICQ

Live Messenger

Skype

Jabber

Yahoo!

Home Phone

Mobile Phone

Work Phone

Update Profile

---

⑧ — Update Profile

Photos

Upload as many photos as you'd like and they will appear on your profile. **Click an image to delete it from your profile.**

⑤ — Add photo through Gravatar...

Links

You can add links to any website you like here and they will be included on your profile.

URL: http://   Title:

⑥ — Add Link

Verified External Services

Verifying an external service helps people to confirm that you are in fact who you say you are. These will all be listed on your public profile.

Add External Service: Blogger ▾   Verify through Gravatar...

⑦

Defining Your Personal Settings

Another item for your to-do list before you start creating your website is to define your personal settings. There are numerous options on the Personal Settings page. In this example, you review the most important settings to consider.

Define Your Personal Settings

① From the main navigation menu, select **Users**, **Personal Settings**.

② Select the **Enable Geotagging** check box if you want to assign a physical location to your posts.

> **IMPORTANT** *Consider carefully whether you want to reveal your physical location before enabling this feature. It's most useful for those who have a business with a physical location, such as a store or restaurant. Travel bloggers can also use this feature to geolocate each post during their travels.*

③ If you don't want to show the feedback and progress sidebar after you post, deselect the **Instant Post Feedback** check box. This sidebar displays by default each time you publish a post, notifying you of its success, enabling you to share your post, and suggesting some additional tags.

④ Select the **Keyboard Shortcuts** check box if you want to use keyboard shortcuts to moderate comments. For example, the letter j selects the next comment, and the letter k moves you back.

⑤ The Twitter API lets you send status updates to your site from a Twitter client. By default, Twitter publishes geolocation data with your updates. If you don't want to share location data, deselect this check box.

6 Select the **Browser Connection** check box to use HTTPS when visiting your admin pages. This adds a layer of security and ensures no one can steal your login credentials or other important data. This is particularly critical if you log in to your WordPress account using a public Wi-Fi connection.

7 In the Proofreading section, you can choose to enable WordPress.com's built-in proofreading technology, which is called After the Deadline, to proofread posts and pages when you publish or update them. In this section, you can also specify the proofreading rules you want to follow, such as checking for passive voice or double negatives.

Did You Know?

HTTPS stands for Hypertext Transfer Protocol Secure and is a communications protocol that ensures secure network communication.

See Also

See "Checking Spelling, Grammar, and Style" in Chapter 8, "Formatting Pages and Posts," for more information about After the Deadline proofreading tools.

6

Browser Connection	☐ Always use HTTPS when visiting administration pages (Learn More)
Interface language	en - English ▼
	You can also specify the language this blog is written in.
Primary Blog	granitecovedesign.wordpress.com ▼
Proofreading	Automatically proofread content when:
	☐ a post or page is first published
	☐ a post or page is updated

English Options

Enable proofreading for the following grammar and style rules when writing posts and pages:

☑ Bias Language
☐ Clichés
☐ Complex Phrases
☐ Diacritical Marks
☐ Double Negatives
☐ Hidden Verbs
☑ Jargon
☑ Passive Voice
☑ Phrases to Avoid
☐ Redundant Phrases

7

8 If you want to use Zemanta to find related content (such as images, links, tags, and related articles) when you create a post, select the **Additional Post Content** check box.

9 In the Account Details section, you can change your username, email address, or password.

10 Click the **Save Changes** button.

Did You Know?

WordPress displays your Zemanta API key on this screen, which you might need if you contact Zemanta for support.

See Also

See Chapter 7, "Creating and Managing Posts," for more information about Zemanta.

Did You Know?

A strong password helps keep your website secure. If you want WordPress to create a strong password for you, click the **Generate Strong Password** button.

Additional Post Content ☑ Help me find related content (images, links, related articles, and tags) to use in my posts. Powered by Zemanta!

Your Zemanta API key is 4n8xcmk9vxokyhh9hdak42tq (you should only need this if you contact Zemanta support and they ask for it)

Account Details

Username   patricer (Change)

E-mail *(required)*   patrice@patricerutledge.com
Used for notifications, not published.

Website   http://globetrottingchef.wordpress.com
Automatically linked when you make comments.

New Password

👁 Hide

🔑 Generate strong password

Learn about choosing great passwords.

Save Changes

Finding and Following Friends

Optionally, you can find and follow friends on WordPress.com just as you follow other interesting topics.

Find and Follow Friends

1. Pause your mouse over your username in the Admin Bar.

2. Click **Find Friends**.

3. Click the **Connect** link to the right of the social site—such as Twitter, Facebook, or Google+—that you want to search for friends who have WordPress.com sites; then follow the connection instructions.

4. WordPress displays friends on WordPress at the bottom of the screen. Click **Follow** to the right of the people you want to follow.

Follow Your Friends

Are your Facebook, Twitter, and Google friends blogging with WordPress? Give the friend finder a whirl to find out.

Twitter   Connect

Facebook   Connect

Google   Connect

We'll display your friends with WordPress blogs here. Try following Matt; he'll be your friend if you do!

Matt Mullenweg

   Follow

WordPress cofounder Matt Mullenweg displays by default

Getting Help

At times you might need additional help in completing an in-progress task or figuring out how to do something that goes beyond the scope of this book. Fortunately, help is just a click away. WordPress continuously updates its help system, so if you're connected to the Web while you search for help, you'll always get the latest support content.

Get Help

1. Pause your mouse over your user-name in the Admin Bar.

2. Click **Help**.

3. WordPress displays its Support page in your browser.

> **TIMESAVER** *Navigate directly to WordPress Support at http://en.support.wordpress.com.*

Did You Know?

You can also get context-sensitive help by clicking the **Help** button on any screen. The screen expands to display relevant help content.

Click a help topic | Search for help on a specific topic

Context-sensitive help | Help button

Verifying Your Website

If you're serious about creating a professional website, you should verify your site with Google Webmaster Tools (https://www.google.com/webmasters/tools) and Bing Webmaster Center (http://www.bing.com/webmaster). If you use Pinterest, you should also verify with Pinterest Site Verification (https://pinterest.com/website/verify). Verifying your site confirms your ownership and gives you access to more tools and features. Each site verification process is different, but all require you to enter a specific meta tag on the Tools screen.

Verify Your Website

1 From the main menu, select **Tools**, **Available Tools**.

2 In the **Google Webmaster Tools** field, enter your Google meta tag.

3 In the **Bing Webmaster Center** field, enter your Bing meta tag.

4 In the **Pinterest Site Verification** field, enter your Pinterest meta tag.

5 Click **Save Changes**.

> **TIMESAVER** *If you aren't familiar with these tools, view http://en.support.wordpress.com/webmaster-tools for step-by-step guidance on completing each verification process.*

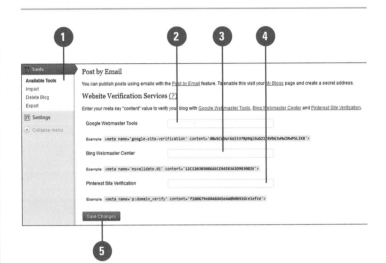

Signing Out of WordPress.com

When you finish working on your website, you can sign out of WordPress.com.

Sign Out of WordPress.com

1. Pause your mouse over your user-name in the Admin Bar.

2. Click **Sign Out**.

   TIMESAVER *If you're working from a computer that only you have access to, you can skip signing out and have WordPress remember you automatically (if you selected Remember Me the last time you signed in).*

Getting Started with WordPress (WordPress.org)

Using self-hosted WordPress gives you complete control over your website, including the capability to use custom themes, install plugins, implement e-commerce functionality, and modify code. If you decide self-hosted WordPress is the right solution for you, this chapter shows you how to get up and running as quickly as possible.

What You'll Do

Install WordPress

Log In to WordPress

Create Your WordPress Profile

Get Help

Log Out of WordPress

Installing WordPress

You can install WordPress from WordPress.org or from an automated installation tool your web host provides. If you don't have strong technical skills, finding a web host that automates WordPress installation is your best bet.

In this example, you install WordPress using the web host HostGator. The steps might vary with a different web host, but the process is similar.

Install WordPress

1. Log in to your HostGator Control Panel.

2. Click the **Fantastico De Luxe** icon.

3. Click **WordPress**.

See Also

See "Understanding Web Hosting" in Chapter 1, "Introducing WordPress," for more information on selecting a web host, including several recommended options.

4. Click the **New Installation** link.

5. In the Installation Location section, select the domain where you want to install WordPress.

6. In the Admin Access Data section, enter a username and password for the account admin.

7. In the Base Configuration section, enter an admin nickname, email address, your site name, and description.

8. Click the **Install WordPress** button.

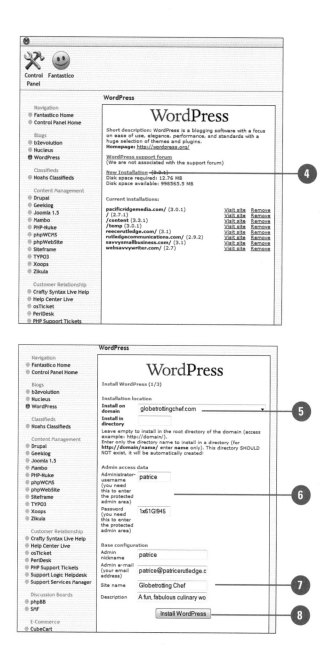

9 Click the **Finish Installation** button.

10 Click the URL to your admin area.

Did You Know?

When you first create a WordPress website, the Dashboard displays tips and information for getting started. Later, WordPress replaces this introductory content with standard Dashboard features, described in the "Exploring the WordPress Dashboard" sidebar later in this chapter.

Did You Know?

Depending on the version of WordPress your web host installs, WordPress might prompt you to install updates.

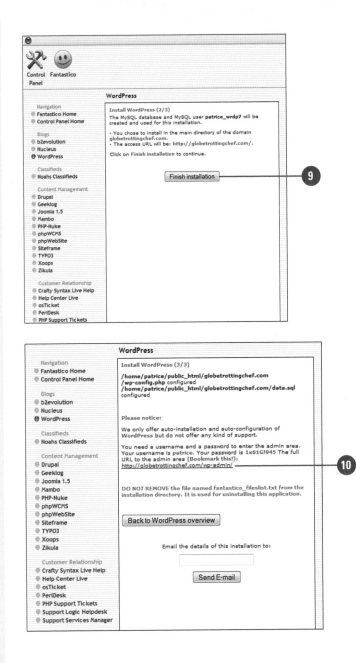

Enter your username and password and click the **Log In** button.

 WordPress displays your Dashboard.

See Also

See "Installing WordPress Updates" in Chapter 18, "Managing Your WordPress Website."

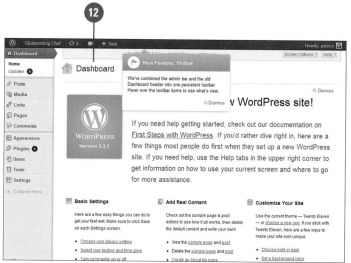

Navigating WordPress

The left side of every WordPress screen includes a vertical navigation menu, divided into sections, that helps you find WordPress features. The selected section displays menu options below its heading. To view menu options for another section, pause your mouse over it. If you decide the menu is taking up too much space, you can collapse it by clicking **Collapse Menu** at the bottom of the menu. This leaves you with only icons as your navigational tool.

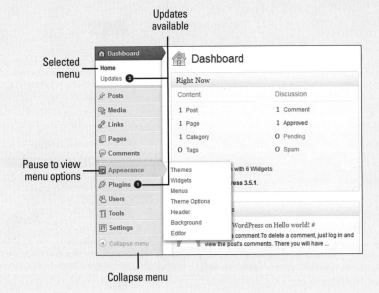

Updates available

Selected menu

Pause to view menu options

Collapse menu

Exploring the WordPress Toolbar

The toolbar displays at the top of the Word-Press screen when you're logged in. On this bar, you can do the following:

- Pause your mouse over the WordPress icon to view a shortcut menu with options to visit the WordPress.org website, view documentation, or access the support forum.

- Click the WordPress icon to view the Word-Press welcome screen.

- Click your site name to view your site in a browser.

- Pause your mouse over the New button to display a shortcut menu to create new content, such as a new post, page, user, and so forth.

- Click the New button to open the Add New Post screen.

- Pause your mouse over your username to view a shortcut menu with options to edit your profile or log out.

- Click your username or Gravatar to open the Profile screen, described in the "Creating Your WordPress Profile" section later in this chapter.

Did You Know?

A Gravatar is a small photo that represents you on the Web. On WordPress, your Gravatar displays next to your posts and comments. If you already have a Gravatar associated with the email address you used to install WordPress, it displays automatically on the toolbar. Otherwise, you can sign up for your own Gravatar at https://en.gravatar.com/site/signup.

See Also

See "Managing Discussion Settings" in Chapter 4, "Specifying WordPress Settings," for more information about using Gravatars with WordPress.

WordPress icon   Updates   Create new post   Gravatar

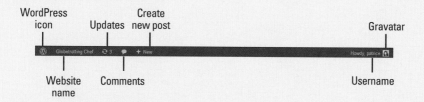

Website name   Comments   Username

Exploring the WordPress Dashboard

When you log in to WordPress, you view the Dashboard. From this WordPress activity hub, you can do the following:

◆ View current information about your posts, pages, and comments in the Right Now box.

◆ Create a basic post using the QuickPress box.

◆ View your recent drafts, comments, and incoming links.

◆ View WordPress news.

Did You Know?

Depending on how you configure WordPress and the plugins you install, your Dashboard content might vary. Click the **Screen Options** button to control what displays on your Dashboard. You can also drag and drop content to rearrange it.

Info about your site   Create a quick post

View recent comments

Manage recent drafts

Logging In to WordPress

Whenever you want to work on your WordPress website, you can log in with your username and password.

Log In to WordPress

1 Navigate to your login screen, such as http://globetrottingchef.com/wp-admin.

2 Enter your username.

3 Enter your password.

4 If you want WordPress to remember your username and password, select the **Remember Me** check box.

   IMPORTANT *If you're logging in from a public computer, you should never have WordPress remember your username and password.*

5 Click the **Log In** button to log in to WordPress.

Did You Know?

If you can't remember your password, click the **Lost Your Password?** link to create a new one. You can also change your password manually on the Profile screen (see the "Creating Your WordPress Profile" section later in this chapter).

Getting Started with WordPress

Setting up a self-hosted WordPress website might seem like a daunting task at first. Here's a simple seven-step plan for getting started.

1. Install the latest WordPress updates. See "Installing WordPress Updates" in Chapter 18.

2. Create your profile. See "Creating Your WordPress Profile" later in this chapter.

3. Specify WordPress settings. See Chapter 4 for more information.

4. Apply a new theme. WordPress comes with a default theme, but most users prefer using a theme that's tailored to their website needs. See Chapter 5, "Working with Themes."

5. Install plugins, which extend the power of WordPress with additional functionality. See Chapter 12, "Working with Plugins (WordPress.org)."

6. Add sidebar content. See Chapter 10, "Working with Widgets."

7. Add and publish your content. See Chapter 6, "Creating and Managing Pages," and Chapter 7, "Creating and Managing Posts."

TIMESAVER *If you followed the guidelines in Chapter 1, you should already have a solid plan that simplifies creating your website.*

Did You Know?

Plugins can enable you to perform site backups, control spam, sell products and services, embed audio and video, display content sliders, create a membership site, enhance your site's SEO, connect with social sites such as Facebook or Twitter, and much more.

Creating Your WordPress Profile

Before you start working on your website itself, you should create your profile. WordPress uses your profile and related Gravatar as a means of identification.

Create Your WordPress Profile

1 From the main navigation menu, select **Users**, **Your Profile**.

> **TIMESAVER** *You can also open the Profile screen by clicking your username on the toolbar.*

2 Select the **Visual Editor** check box if you want to disable the Visual Editor when creating posts and pages.

> **IMPORTANT** *The Visual Editor is the default editing mode for WordPress; it enables you to enter and format content using a view similar to a word processing application such as Microsoft Word. If you disable this, you must use the Text Editor, in which you can edit your content's HTML. Unless you have a strong reason for disabling the Visual Editor, you should ignore this field.*

3 Select your preferred **Admin Color Scheme**: blue or gray (the default).

4 Select the **Keyboard Shortcuts** check box if you want to use keyboard shortcuts to moderate comments. For example, the letter j selects the next comment, and the letter k moves you back.

5 By default, WordPress displays the toolbar at the top of screen. If you don't want to display this, deselect the **Toolbar** check box.

6 In the Name section, enter your username, first name, last name, nickname, and display name (the name that displays next to your posts).

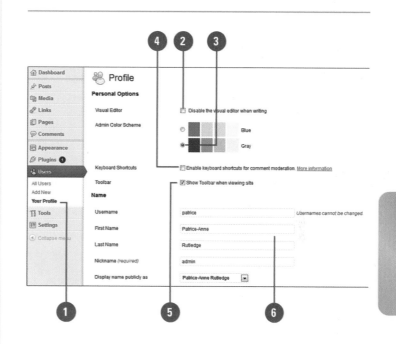

7 In the Contact Info section, enter your email address (this should default to the address you used when you set up the account) and, optionally, your website or any instant message accounts.

8 Enter information about yourself in the Biographical Info box.

9 If you want to change the password you chose at signup, enter a new password twice.

10 Click the **Update Profile** button.

Did You Know?

The Strength Indicator field lets you know how strong your password is. A good password should contain at least seven characters and include both uppercase and lowercase letters, numbers, and symbols (such as !, ?, and so forth).

See Also

If you aren't the only person contributing content to your site, see Chapter 16, "Managing Users," to learn more about adding more users.

7

Contact Info

E-mail *(required)*   patrice@patricerutledge.com

Website

AIM

Yahoo IM

Jabber / Google Talk

About Yourself

Biographical Info

Share a little biographical information to fill out your profile. This may be shown publicly.

8

9

New Password   *If you would like to change the password type a new one. Otherwise leave this blank.*

Type your new password again.

Strength Indicator   *Hint: The password should be at least seven characters long. To make it stronger, use upper and lower case letters, numbers and symbols like ! " ? $ % ^ &).*

Update Profile

10

Getting Help

There are times when you might need additional help in completing an in-progress task or figuring out how to do something that goes beyond the scope of this book. Fortunately, help is a click away.

Get Help

1. Click the **Help** button in the upper-right corner of the screen.

2. The screen expands to display relevant help content.

   TIMESAVER *Navigate directly to WordPress Support at http:// wordpress.org/support.*

View WordPress documentation

Go to support forums

Click to collapse help

Logging Out of WordPress

When you finish working on your website, you can log out of WordPress.

Log Out of WordPress

1 Pause your mouse over your username on the toolbar.

2 Click **Log Out**.

> **TIMESAVER** *If you're working from a computer that only you have access to, you can skip logging out and have WordPress remember you automatically (if you selected Remember Me the last time you logged in).*

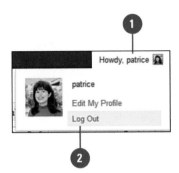

Specifying WordPress Settings

WordPress offers a variety of settings that enable you to control all aspects of your website. Although it might seem like extra work to review numerous settings when you're eager to start adding content to your site, it can pay off in the long run. By customizing your WordPress settings, often a one-time task, you can better manage your site, receive only the notifications you want, and avoid any unpleasant surprises.

Although most WordPress settings are selected by default and require action only if you want to change them, a few require you to enter specific information to set up your initial site. Throughout this chapter, I indicate where it's important for you to take action, which settings you just need to review, and when settings differ depending on whether you're using WordPress.org or WordPress.com.

What You'll Do

Specify General Settings

Specify Writing Settings

Specify Reading Settings

Manage Discussion Settings

Modify Media Settings

Customize Permalinks Settings (WordPress.org)

Enable Sharing (WordPress.com)

Set Up Polls (WordPress.com)

Set Up Ratings (WordPress.com)

Specify Email Post Changes Settings (WordPress.com)

Add OpenID Trusted Sites (WordPress.com)

Add Webhooks (WordPress.com)

Specifying General Settings

The General Settings screen helps you get started with WordPress. In particular, you should verify that your site title, tagline, email address, and time zone are accurate.

Specify General Settings

1. From the main navigation menu, select **Settings**, **General**.

2. By default, WordPress displays the site title you entered during setup. If you want to change this, enter a new title in the **Site Title** field.

3. Enter a brief **Tagline** that describes what your site is about.

4. (WordPress.org) Your site's WordPress Address and Site Address default from setup. If you want your website's home page URL to differ from the directory in which you installed WordPress, enter that URL in the **Site Address (URL)** field.

   IMPORTANT *Don't change these URLs unless you fully understand the ramifications of doing so. For more information, see http://codex.wordpress.org/ Giving_WordPress_Its_Own_ Directory.*

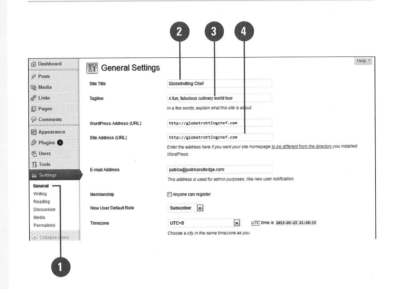

Did You Know?

WordPress displays your site title and tagline on your browser's title bar. Depending on the theme you installed, these fields might also display at the top of every page on your site unless you replace them with a logo. Your site title also displays on your feed.

⑤ Enter the **E-mail Address** you want WordPress to use for site notifications. If you enter a new email address, you must confirm it before WordPress begins notifying you.

⑥ (WordPress.org) If you want to enable others to register for an account on your site, select the **Membership** check box.

⑦ (WordPress.org) Select the **New User Default Role** from the drop-down list. Your choices include Subscriber (the default), Administrator, Editor, Author, or Contributor.

⑧ Select your **Timezone** from the drop-down list. You can select a time offset from the UTC (Coordinated Universal Time) or scroll up and select a major city in your time zone, such as Los Angeles or Chicago.

IMPORTANT *Selecting your time zone is important if you plan to schedule your posts. For example, if you want to post at 8:00 a.m. every Thursday and you live in San Francisco, you need to set up WordPress to use your time zone. Otherwise, your post could become active at the wrong time, such as in the middle of the night.*

See Also

See Chapter 16, "Managing Users" for more information about user roles.

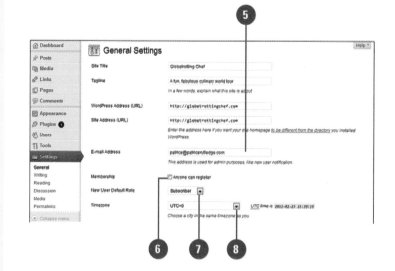

For Your Information

Consider Carefully Who Can Post on Your Site

Letting others post on your site is a powerful tool. Be sure you think carefully about who can post on your site and what rights they should have. Before adding new users, you should have a thorough understanding of WordPress user roles, know the rights provided with each role, and select the appropriate default role for new users.

9 Select the **Date Format** you want to display on your posts.

10 Select the **Time Format** you want to display on your posts.

11 Select the first day of the week from the **Week Starts On** drop-down list.

12 (WordPress.com) Select your site's primary **Language**. The default is English.

13 (WordPress.com) To upload a picture (JPEG or PNG) to use as your blog image, click the **Browse** button, select a picture, and click the **Upload Image** button. Optionally, you can crop your image to suit your needs.

TIMESAVER *What if you don't like the image you uploaded? Click the **Remove Image** button and start over.*

14 Click **Save Changes**.

Date Format	● July 5, 2012	**9**
	○ 2012/07/05	
	○ 07/05/2012	
	○ 05/07/2012	
	○ Custom: F j, Y July 5, 2012	
	Documentation on date and time formatting.	
Time Format	● 11:49 pm	**10**
	○ 11:49 PM	
	○ 23:49	
	○ Custom: g:i a 11:49 pm	
Week Starts On	Monday ▼	**11**
Language	en - English ▼	**12**
	Language this blog is primarily written in.	
	You can also modify the interface language in your profile.	

Save Changes

14

Blog Picture / Icon

Upload a picture (**jpeg** or **png**) to be used as your blog image across WordPress.com. We will let you crop it after you upload.

[   ] Browse... ———— **13**

Upload Image »

Specifying Writing Settings

The Writing Settings screen offers several options that simplify your WordPress publishing experience. If you don't plan to use the Press This bookmarklet, post by email, or publish remotely, however, you might not need to modify many settings on this screen.

Specify Writing Settings

1. From the main navigation menu, select **Settings, Writing**.

2. By default, WordPress converts text-based emoticons to graphic icons automatically. For example, when you type :-), WordPress displays a smiley face: ☺. If you don't want WordPress to convert emoticons automatically, deselect the **Convert Emoticons Like :-) and :-P to Graphics on Display** check box.

3. Select the **WordPress Should Correct Invalidly Nested XHTML Automatically** check box if you want WordPress to perform this check. This is an important feature to activate if you create posts using the HTML tab and want to be sure that the content you enter here displays correctly on the Web.

4. Select a **Default Post Category** to assign new posts to a specific category automatically. By default, WordPress assigns your posts to the Uncategorized category.

5. Select a **Default Post Format** to assign new posts automatically. By default, WordPress assigns new posts to the Standard category, but you can also choose from the following post types: Aside, Link, Gallery, Status, Quote, or Image.

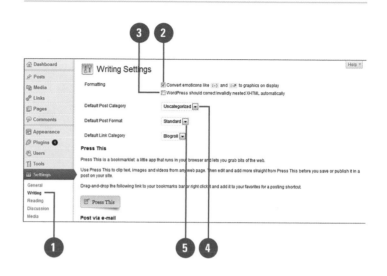

See Also

See "Managing Categories" in Chapter 7, "Creating and Managing Posts," for more information about setting up and managing WordPress categories.

6 Select a **Default Link Category** to assign new links to a specific category automatically. By default, WordPress assigns new links to the Blogroll category.

7 If you want to use the Press This bookmarklet, drag the **Press This** button to your browser's Bookmarks toolbar. The Press This bookmarklet is useful if you want to select web content, such as text, images, or videos, and paste them into a Word-Press post or page quickly.

8 (WordPress.org) If you want to post to your WordPress site by email, set up an email account for this purpose and enter its Mail Server, Login Name, and Password in the **Post via E-mail** section. Optionally, you can also specify a default category for posts WordPress receives by email.

IMPORTANT *To set up posting by email on WordPress.com, select* ***My Blogs*** *from the main navigation menu and click the* ***Enable*** *button for the Post by Email field. WordPress creates a secret address for you to use; there is no need to set one up yourself.*

See Also
See Chapter 7 for more information about post formats.

See Also
See Chapter 11, "Working with Links," for more information.

Writing Settings

Formatting
- ☑ Convert emoticons like :-) and :-P to graphics on display
- ☐ WordPress should correct invalidly nested XHTML, automatically

Default Post Category — Uncategorized
Default Post Format — Standard
Default Link Category — Blogroll

Press This

Press This is a bookmarklet: a little app that runs in your browser and lets you grab bits of the web.

Use Press This to clip text, images and videos from any web page. Then edit and add more straight from Press This before you save or publish it in a post on your site.

Drag-and-drop the following link to your bookmarks bar or right click it and add it to your favorites for a posting shortcut.

[Press This]

Post via e-mail

Post via e-mail

To post to WordPress by e-mail you must set up a secret e-mail account with POP3 access. Any mail received at this address will be posted, so it's a good idea to keep this address very secret. Here are three random strings you could use: juiOAyFM , JuO8uQ18 , ripU2K6d .

Mail Server — mail.example.com — Port 110
Login Name — login@example.com
Password — password
Default Mail Category — Uncategorized

Update Services

When you publish a new post, WordPress automatically notifies the following site update services. For more about this, see Update Services on the Codex. Separate multiple service URLs with line breaks.

http://rpc.pingomatic.com/

[Save Changes]

Did You Know?

Although posting via email can be useful, be aware that this feature requires some planning and setup to implement. You must create a secret email account on your mail server (not an email account with a site such as Gmail, Yahoo!, or Hotmail) and configure it to work with WordPress. For more information, see http://codex.wordpress.org/ Post_to_your_blog_using_email.

9 (WordPress.org) When you publish a new post, WordPress uses the update service Ping-O-Matic (http://rpc.pingomatic.com) to notify multiple search engines that your site has new content. For example, this service notifies Google Blog Search, My Yahoo!, FeedBurner, and other sites. If you want to notify other update services, you can add them to the **Update Services** field. Although Ping-o-Matic is usually sufficient for most sites, you can find a list of other update services to add at http://codex.wordpress.org/Update_Services.

IMPORTANT *The Update Services field isn't available if you blocked search engines on the Reading Settings screen.*

10 Click **Save Changes**.

Post via e-mail

To post to WordPress by e-mail you must set up a secret e-mail account with POP3 access. Any mail received at this address will be posted, so it's a good idea to keep this address very secret. Here are three random strings you could use: `juiOAyfN` , `JxO8uQ15` , `r1pUZK6d` .

| Mail Server | mail.example.com | Port | 110 |

| Login Name | login@example.com |

| Password | password |

| Default Mail Category | Uncategorized [▾] |

Update Services

When you publish a new post, WordPress automatically notifies the following site update services. For more about this, see Update Services on the Codex. Separate multiple service URLs with line breaks.

```
http://rpc.pingomatic.com/
```

Save Changes

10   **9**

Did You Know?

Ping-O-Matic is just one way to notify the world about your new posts. Other ways to get visibility for your content include enabling the PingShot feature in FeedBurner (if you use this tool to burn your feed) and installing the Google XML Sitemaps plugin.

Did You Know?

WordPress.com doesn't include an Update Services field because it updates search engines automatically. Note that you must enable search engine visibility on the Reading Settings screen to activate this feature. WordPress.com sites also include a built-in XML Sitemap for Search Engines.

Specifying Reading Settings

Reading settings enable you to control the appearance of your site's front page, the number of posts you display, and the appearance of your feed. If you want to display something other than a series of posts on your front page, you'll want to customize the settings on the Reading Settings screen.

Specify Reading Settings

① From the main navigation menu, select **Settings, Reading**.

② Specify what you want to display on your front page: **Your Latest Posts** (traditional blog format) or **A Static Page**. If you choose A Static Page, select your **Front Page** and **Posts Page** from the drop-down lists. For example, you might want to create a page named Welcome for your front page and a page named Blog for your posts page.

③ In the **Blog Pages Show at Most** field, enter how many posts you want to display on your posts page. By default, WordPress displays 10 posts.

④ In the **Syndication Feeds Show the Most Recent** field, enter the number of items you want to display in your feed. By default, WordPress displays 10 items.

⑤ For each article in your website's feed, specify how much content you want to show: **Full Text** or **Summary**.

⑥ (WordPress.org) Select the **Discourage Search Engines from Indexing This Site** check box if you don't want WordPress to submit your site to search engines.

Did You Know?

You can syndicate your WordPress posts and content with a feed, making it available for users to subscribe to and view with feed reader applications. The standard feed icon is a small orange square with white radio waves that you can display on your website. Site visitors can click this icon to subscribe to your feed.

7 (WordPress.com) In the Site Visibility section, select your preference for search engine visibility: **Allow Search Engines to Index This Site** or **Discourage Search Engines from Indexing This Site.**

IMPORTANT *Asking search engines not to index doesn't hide your website. It just means that your site won't display in search results. If you want to hide your site completely, create a private site (WordPress.com) or install a privacy plugin (WordPress.org), such as Absolute Privacy (http://wordpress.org/extend/plugins/absolute-privacy/). This is particularly useful when you're first creating your website and it's not ready for public viewing yet.*

8 (WordPress.com) If you want to create a private site, select the **I Would Like My Site to Be Private, Visible Only to Users I Choose** option button. This creates a password-protected site that only authorized users can view. If you choose this option, WordPress prompts you to invite authorized users to your site after you save your changes. If you don't invite anyone, only you can access and view your site.

9 (WordPress.com) By default, WordPress scrolls infinitely as visitors read the content on your site, showing seven posts on each load. To deactivate this feature, deselect the **Scroll Infinitely** check box.

10 (WordPress.com) In the Enhanced Feeds section, select any of the following check boxes to add them to each article in your feed: **Categories**, **Tags**, **Comment Count**, or **Sharing**.

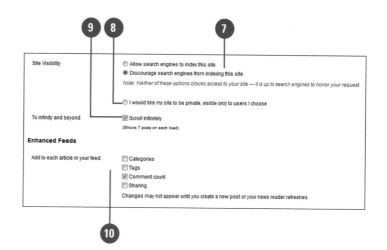

11 (WordPress.com) WordPress displays a Follow button in the upper-left corner of every site, which enables anyone who visits your site to follow it. If you want to allow only registered WordPress.com users to follow you, deselect the **Show Follow Button to Logged Out Users** check box.

TIMESAVER *To customize the email WordPress sends to people who follow you, update the* **Blog Follow Email Text** *and* **Comment Follow Email Text** *boxes.*

12 Click **Save Changes**.

11

Follower Settings

These settings change emails sent from your blog to followers.

Logged out users   ☑ Show follow button to logged out users.

Checking this will present a follow button to logged out users in the bottom corner of their screen.

Blog follow email text

> Howdy,
>
> You recently signed up to follow this blog's posts. This means once you confirm below, you will receive each new post by email.
>
> To activate, click Confirm Follow. If you believe this is an error, ignore this message and nothing more

Introduction text sent when someone follows your blog. (Site and confirmation details will be automatically added for you.)

Comment follow email text

> Howdy,
>
> You recently signed up to follow one of my posts. This means once you confirm below, you will receive an email when new comments are posted.
>
> To activate, click confirm below. If you believe this is an error, ignore this message and nothing more

Introduction text sent when someone follows a post on your blog. (Site and confirmation details will be automatically added for you.)

Save Changes

12

Managing Discussion Settings

The Discussion Settings screen enables you to control the following:

◆ Comment settings

◆ Pingbacks and trackbacks

◆ Comment email notifications

◆ Comment spam

◆ Comment moderation and approval

◆ Comment blacklists

◆ The appearance of avatars in your site's comments section

For most people, the default settings are acceptable, but you should take a few minutes to review them so that you understand these defaults and can modify anything you don't like.

Manage Discussion Settings

1. From the main navigation menu, select **Settings, Discussion**.

2. Review the default discussion settings and modify any setting you want to change.

TIMESAVER *If your Word-Press site is very active and has lots of reader activity, you might not want to receive an email every time someone comments, follows, likes, or reblogs. To avoid notification overwhelm, deselect any of the check boxes in the* ***E-Mail Me Whenever*** *section.*

See Also

See "Creating a Post" in Chapter 7 for more information on pingbacks and trackbacks, which enable you to notify another website when you mention their content in one of your posts.

3 WordPress displays an avatar of each person who comments on your site. If you don't want to display avatars, deselect the **Show Avatars** check box.

4 (WordPress.com) When you mouse over someone's Gravatar, Word-Press displays a hovercard with profile information. To disable this feature, deselect the check box in the **Gravatar Hovercards** field.

5 If your avatar isn't suitable for all audiences, select the appropriate rating option in the **Maximum Rating** field.

6 Select a **Default Avatar** for people who comment but don't have an avatar.

7 Click **Save Changes**.

Did You Know?

An avatar is a small photo that represents you on the Web. WordPress offers its own spin on the traditional avatar: a Gravatar (short for globally recognized avatar). On WordPress, your Gravatar displays next to your posts and comments on both your own site as well as other WordPress sites. You can sign up for your own Gravatar at https://en.gravatar.com/site/signup/.

Avatars

An avatar is an image that follows you from weblog to weblog appearing beside your name when you comment on avatar enabled sites. Here you can enable the display of avatars for people who comment on your site.

Avatar Display	☑ Show Avatars
Gravatar Hovercards	☑ View people's profiles when you mouse over their Gravatars
	Put your mouse over your Gravatar to check out your profile.
Maximum Rating	⦿ G — Suitable for all audiences
	○ PG — Possibly offensive, usually for audiences 13 and above
	○ R — Intended for adult audiences above 17
	○ X — Even more mature than above
Default Avatar	For users without a custom avatar of their own, you can either display a generic logo or a generated one based on their e-mail address.
	○ Mystery Man
	○ Blank
	○ Gravatar Logo
	⦿ Identicon (Generated)
	○ Wavatar (Generated)

Default Avatar	For users without a custom avatar of their own, you can either display a generic logo or a generated one based on their e-mail address.
	⦿ Mystery Man
	○ Blank
	○ Gravatar Logo
	○ Identicon (Generated)
	○ Wavatar (Generated)
	○ MonsterID (Generated)
	○ Retro (Generated)

Save Changes

Modifying Media Settings

Media settings enable you to determine image sizing and control how WordPress embeds and uploads media content. The defaults work well for most people, but you might want to tweak these settings if you have a design background and require more precise control of your media content.

Modify Media Settings

1. From the main navigation menu, select **Settings, Media**.

2. In the **Image Sizes** section, update the maximum sizes of thumbnail, medium, and large images if you don't want to use the default settings.

3. (WordPress.org) WordPress stores your media files in folders identified with a month and year, such as http://patricerutledge.com/wp-uploads/2012/07/image.jpg. If you don't want to add the month and year to your folder path, remove the check mark next to the **Organize My Uploads into Month- and Year-Based Folders** check box.

Did You Know?

A thumbnail is a reduced-size version of an image. Many WordPress themes use thumbnails on pages that display excerpts of multiple posts (such as a home page or blog page) or on post-related widgets.

4 (WordPress.com) In the **Image Gallery Carousel** section, specify whether you want to display images in a carousel slideshow and, if so, which carousel features you want to use. This feature is enabled by default.

5 In the **Video Player** section, optionally specify whether you want to display only videos in free software formats.

6 Click **Save Changes**.

See Also

See Chapter 9, "Working with Media Files," for more information about the image gallery carousel.

See Also

See Chapter 9 for more information about inserting videos into your posts and pages and Chapter 15, "Using WordPress.com Premium Features," for more information about purchasing the VideoPress upgrade.

4

Media Settings `Hel`

Image sizes

The sizes listed below determine the maximum dimensions in pixels to use when inserting an image into the body of a post.

Thumbnail size — Width `150` Height `150`

Medium size — Max Width `300` Max Height `300`

Large size — Max Width `1024` Max Height `1024`

Image Gallery Carousel

Enable carousel — ☑ Display images in full-size carousel slideshow.

Background color — Black ▾

Metadata — ☑ Show photo metadata (Exif) in carousel, when available.

Tiled Galleries — ☐ Display all your gallery pictures in a cool mosaic.

Video player

Free formats — ☐ Only display videos in free software formats

Ogg file container with Theora video and Vorbis audio. Note that some browsers are unable to play free software video formats, including Internet Explorer and Safari.

Save Changes

6   **5**

Customizing Permalinks Settings (WordPress.org)

The Permalink Settings screen enables you to create a custom structure for your site's permalinks.

Customize Permalinks Settings

1. From the main navigation menu, select **Settings, Permalinks**.

2. In the **Common Settings** section, select the permalinks structure you prefer. The most popular structures include the post name.

3. Click **Save Changes**.

Did You Know?

A permalink is a permanent URL that corresponds to an individual post or page on your website. When others link to a post on your site, they use its permalink. The default permalink structure looks like this: http://patricerutledge.com/?p=123. Not particularly informative, is it? Fortunately, WordPress gives you the option of changing your permalink structure to something more user friendly, such as http://patricerutledge.com/2012/11/favorite-wordpress-plugins.

Enabling Sharing (WordPress.com)

The Sharing Settings screen enables you to share your posts automatically on other social sites and add buttons that let readers easily share their favorite posts and pages from your site.

In the Publicize section of this screen, you can connect your WordPress.com site to many popular social networking sites and share your posts automatically. Supported sites include Facebook, Twitter, LinkedIn, Tumblr, and Yahoo!. For example, you could click the **Add New Twitter Connection** link to connect WordPress to your Twitter account. The next time you post something on WordPress, a link to it displays on your Twitter profile.

IMPORTANT *You can add the Publicize feature to a self-hosted WordPress site with the Jetpack plugin (http:// wordpress.org/extend/plugins/jetpack). Numerous other social sharing plugins are also available, if Publicize doesn't meet your needs.*

Enable Sharing

1. From the main navigation menu, select **Settings**, **Sharing**.

2. Click the link next to a social site to connect WordPress to this account.

3. Specify which sharing buttons you want to display on your site using the options in the **Sharing Buttons** section. By default, WordPress has enabled the Press This, Twitter, and Facebook buttons, but you can also add buttons for Email, Print, Digg, LinkedIn, Reddit, StumbleUpon, Google +1, Tumblr, and Pinterest. To enable a service, drag its button from the **Available Services** section to the **Enabled Services** section.

   TIMESAVER *What if you don't want to display a button anymore? Just drag it back from the Enabled Services section to the Available Services section.*

See Also

See Appendix B, "WordPress Plugins (WordPress.org)," for a list of recommended social sharing plugins.

4 Select a **Button Style** from the following options: Icon+ Text, Icon Only, Text Only, or Official Buttons.

5 Enter a **Sharing Label**. By default, WordPress displays "Share This:" as the label. You can also remove this text if you don't want to display any label.

6 From the **Open Links In** drop-down list, specify whether you want to open links in the same window or a new window. If you want to keep visitors on your site, opening a new window is the best option.

7 In the **Show Buttons On** section, specify where you want to display your buttons. Your options include the following:

- Front Page, Archive Pages, and Search Results
- Posts
- Pages
- Media

8 By default, WordPress.com displays Likes on all posts. Optionally, you can enable this feature per post by selecting the **Turned on per Post** option button.

9 Click **Save Changes**.

Button style	Icon + text
Sharing label	Share this:
Open links in	Same window
Show buttons on	☐ Front Page, Archive Pages, and Search Results ☑ Posts ☑ Pages ☐ Media
WordPress.com Likes are	● On for all posts ○ Turned on per post

Save Changes

Setting Up Polls (WordPress.com)

On the Poll Settings screen you can enable polls and ratings on your website by importing your Polldaddy (http://polldaddy.com/) account into WordPress and specifying poll settings.

Set Up the Polling Feature

1 From the main navigation menu, select **Settings**, **Polls**.

IMPORTANT *If you use self-hosted WordPress, the Poll Settings screen isn't available. Instead, you can use the Polldaddy Polls & Ratings plugin to enable polls and ratings on your website (http://wordpress.org/extend/plugins/polldaddy/).*

2 Enter your **Polldaddy Email Address** and **Polldaddy Password**.

3 Click the **Import Account** button.

4 In the **General Settings** section, specify the default poll settings you want to use, such as default poll settings, your preferred poll style, and more.

5 Click **Save Options**.

See Also

See "Adding a Poll" in Chapter 14, "Getting Feedback on Your Website (WordPress.com)," to learn more about using polls in WordPress.com.

Setting Up Ratings (WordPress.com)

Ratings offer a great way to get feedback on your website content. WordPress enables your readers to rate posts, pages, and comments. (You control which, if any, of these are available and able to rate.) You can use the default rating options (Very Poor, Poor, Average, Good, or Excellent) or create your own. On the Rating Settings screen you can enable ratings and specify the exact rating features you want to use.

Enable Ratings

1. From the main navigation menu, select **Settings**, **Ratings**.

2. Click the **Posts** tab to enable ratings and specify rating positioning on your posts.

3. Click the **Pages** tab to enable ratings and specify rating positioning on your pages.

4. Click the **Comments** tab to enable ratings and specify rating positioning on your comments.

5. Click **Save Changes**.

See Also

See Chapter 14 for more information about viewing and managing ratings.

Did You Know?

Click the **Advanced Settings** link to display an extensive list of additional options. For example, you can specify your preferred rating style, text, layout, labels, and more.

Specifying Email Post Changes Settings (WordPress.com)

On the Email Post Changes screen, you can specify whether you want WordPress.com to notify you anytime a user makes a change to a post or page on your site.

Specify Email Post Changes Settings

1. From the main navigation menu, select **Settings**, **Email Post Changes**.

2. Select the **Send an Email When a Post or Page Changes** check box if you want to enable the Email Post Changes feature.

3. In the **Users to Email** field, select the check box next to the users you want WordPress to notify by email.

4. In the **Additional Email Addresses** box, enter the email addresses of any additional people you want to notify who aren't users of this WordPress account.

5. Specify whether you want to receive email notifications for **Posts**, **Pages**, or both.

6. Select the **Email Changes to Drafts, Not Just Published Items** check box if you want to receive email notification about drafts.

7. Click **Save Changes**.

TIMESAVER *Receiving emails about post changes is particularly useful on a multiuser site where you want to keep track of what your users are posting.*

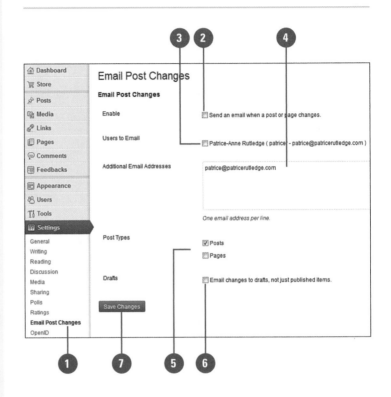

Adding OpenID Trusted Sites (WordPress.com)

On the OpenID Settings screen, you can view your OpenID and add trusted sites that you can access with this ID.

Add an OpenID Trusted Site

1 From the main navigation menu, select **Settings**, **OpenID**.

2 Enter the URL of a trusted site that supports OpenID in the **Site URL** field.

3 Click **Add Site**. WordPress adds the site to your trusted site list, and that site won't prompt you to confirm that you trust the site when you log in.

Did You Know?

OpenID is an open standard that enables you to log in to other websites using a common identifying URL. Your WordPress.com URL doubles as an OpenID, giving you easy access to many popular sites. For example, if your WordPress URL is http://globetrottingchef.wordpress.com, this URL also functions as an OpenID. You can find a list of websites that support OpenID at https://www.myopenid.com/directory.

TIMESAVER To remove a site from the trusted site list, select its check box and click the **Delete** button.

Adding Webhooks (WordPress.com)

On the Webhooks screen, you can add and manage webhooks, which enable you to develop your own custom notifications. For example, you could add a webhook for comment or post notifications. Although webhooks are useful for developers and advanced users, the average WordPress user is unlikely to use webhooks. If you're technically savvy or just curious, you can learn more about webhooks at http://en.support.wordpress.com/webhooks/.

Add a Webhook

1 From the main navigation menu, select **Settings**, **Webhooks**.

2 Click the **Add Webhook** button.

3 In the Add New Webhook dialog box, select an **Action** and one or more **Fields**, enter a **URL**, and click the **Add New Webhook** button.

Working with Themes

One of the most important elements of any WordPress website is its theme. A theme controls the appearance of your site and is a framework for your own content, such as pages, posts, and media files. A theme isn't a single file, but rather a collection of files including the following elements:

- One or more stylesheets that control your site's appearance. Style sheets use Cascading Style Sheets (CSS) to specify a theme's exact layout, fonts, color, and other design elements. The main theme stylesheet in all WordPress themes is named style.css.

- Image files (*.jpg, *.gif, *.png).

- Template and function files (with the extension *.php) that control the content on pages, single posts, index pages, comments, and other functionality.

IMPORTANT *If you aren't technical, don't worry about working with these files—just be aware of their role in your theme. If you're eager to get into the technical intricacies of WordPress, however, you can customize your style sheet using CSS or make other code modifications.*

What You'll Do

Search for and Activate a Theme (WordPress.com)

Search for and Install a Theme (WordPress.org)

Search for Themes in the WordPress Free Themes Directory (WordPress.org)

Upload a Theme (WordPress.org)

Use Live Preview

Activate a Different Theme

Customize Your Theme

Delete a Theme (WordPress.org)

Understanding Theme Differences Between WordPress.org and WordPress.com

When you first set up a self-hosted website, WordPress installs the Twenty Eleven theme by default. Although this is a quality theme, you should explore other options before making your final theme choice. When you create a website on WordPress.com, you're prompted to select a starter theme or accept the default theme. Although themes are essentially the same no matter which version of WordPress you use to create your site, some distinct differences exist as well.

WordPress.org	WordPress.com
Search for and install free themes from the Manage Themes screen	Search for and install both free and premium themes from the Manage Themes screen
Upload external themes downloaded from the Web, including premium themes	Can't upload external themes from the Web
Customize themes using screens available for your active theme	Customize themes using the Theme Customizer or one of the following screens: Theme Options, Custom Header, or Custom Background
Customize theme design, fonts, and CSS using the Edit Themes screen	Customize theme design, fonts, and CSS by purchasing the Custom Design upgrade
Delete installed themes you don't want	Can't delete themes because you don't install them

Exploring WordPress Theme Layout Options

Determining the type of website you want to create can help you narrow options and select the perfect theme. Although all themes share certain common elements, choosing a theme that matches the intended focus of your site helps you get up and running much faster. Here are four of the most common types of WordPress themes:

◆ **Blog**—The blog format is the original WordPress layout and is still one of the most popular for displaying a series of sequential blog posts on your site's home page. Optionally, you can choose to display a static page as your home page and make your blog available from a link on a menu or sidebar.

◆ **Magazine**—Magazine layouts enable you to display multiple posts, photos, and videos on your home page and work best for content-driven sites.

◆ **Portfolio**—Portfolio themes showcase sample projects and are popular with creative professionals such as designers, photographers, and writers.

◆ **E-commerce**—E-commerce themes are designed for online stores or other websites that offer products for sale.

Exploring WordPress Theme Pricing Options

WordPress themes are available in a variety of price ranges. Your options include the following:

◆ **Free themes**—With thousands of free themes available, the hardest part is choosing just one. You can find free themes by searching the Manage Themes screen within WordPress. If you use WordPress.org, also check out the WordPress Free Themes Directory at http://wordpress.org/extend/themes. Although the price is right with free themes, you might require more flexibility, features, or support for your business or professional site.

◆ **Premium themes**—Premium themes offer advanced features not found in most free themes and often include technical support and updates. Most premium themes are priced below $100, so the investment might be worthwhile if you're creating a site for business.

◆ **Custom themes**—The most expensive option is a custom-designed theme that you can upload to your WordPress.org site. If you want a theme that's unique only to your site, a custom theme is the way to go. Keep in mind, however, that hiring an experienced designer to create a custom theme can be pricey.

See Also

See Appendix A, "WordPress.org Premium Themes," for more information about premium themes you can use on WordPress.org sites.

Five Steps to Choosing the Perfect Theme

Now that you have some idea about the types of theme layouts and price ranges available, it's time to start searching for a theme for your site. Here are a few great tips for choosing the perfect theme:

1. **Define the theme features and design elements you need.** Although you can customize a theme, it's best to choose one that already meets most of your requirements rather than spending too much time on customization. This is particularly important if you're a Word-Press beginner and don't have experience modifying themes. For example, determine the layout you require, how many sidebars you want, your color preferences, any special elements you need (such as sliders or galleries), and so forth.

2. **Determine your theme budget.** See "Exploring WordPress Theme Pricing Options" earlier in this chapter for more information.

3. **Search for themes that match your criteria.** Narrowing your initial choices to three to five potential themes helps you avoid the overwhelming task of scrolling through thousands of options.

4. **Take potential themes on a test drive.** Installing a free theme and trying it out is easy, but analyzing premium themes can be a bit tricky. Fortunately, many premium theme developers give you hands-on access to their themes before you buy.

5. **Select a theme and activate it.** Optionally, you might have to purchase or download the theme before activation, depending on your choice of theme.

If you're lucky, your first choice of theme works out perfectly. But if you're like most people, you'll try out multiple themes before settling on the one you want to use on your published site.

Searching for and Activating a Theme (WordPress.com)

On WordPress.com, you must search for and activate all themes on the Manage Themes screen.

Search for and Activate a Theme

1 From the main navigation menu, select **Appearance**, **Themes**.

2 Click the **Feature Filter** link.

TIMESAVER *Optionally, click one of the following links to view themes that match these criteria:* ***Popular***, ***Newest***, ***Premium***, *or* ***Friends of WP.com***. *Another option is to enter keywords and click the* ***Search*** *button to display matches.*

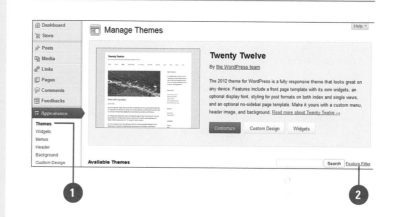

3 Select the check boxes next to the theme features you want. You can filter by color, number of columns, sidebar location, width, or other features, such as only themes that support custom headers, custom menus, or featured images.

4 Click the **Apply Filters** button at the bottom of the screen. WordPress displays thumbnails of all themes that match your criteria.

5 Scroll down the screen and click the **Live Preview** link below a theme's thumbnail to preview it. When you're finished previewing, click the **Close** button (x) in the upper-left corner of the preview window to close it and return to your list of matching themes.

6 Click the **Details** link below a theme's thumbnail to view more information about a theme, including its version number and user rating.

7 If you want to activate a free theme, click the **Activate** link below the theme's thumbnail.

8 If you want to activate a premium theme, click the **Purchase** link below the theme's thumbnail. The theme's price displays next to the link. WordPress prompts you to pay for the theme by credit card or PayPal.

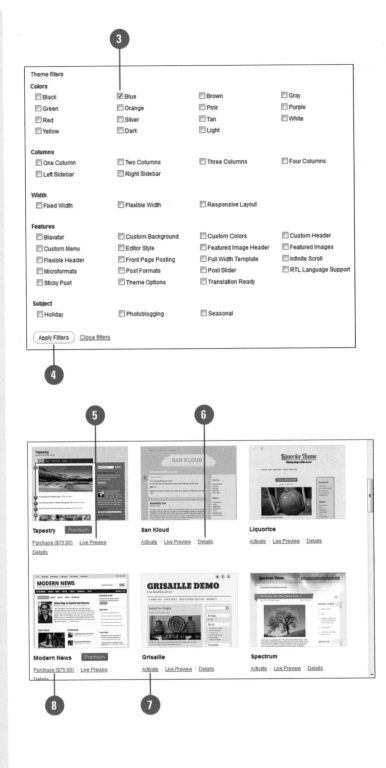

Searching for and Installing a Theme (WordPress.org)

If you use self-hosted WordPress, one way to find a new theme is to search the themes directory on the Install Themes screen.

Search for and Install a Theme

1. From the main navigation menu, select **Appearance**, **Themes**.

2. Click the **Install Themes** tab.

3. Select the check boxes next to the theme features you want. You can filter by color, number of columns, sidebar location, width, or other features, such as only themes that support custom headers, custom menus, or featured images.

   TIMESAVER *Optionally, click one of the following links to view themes that match these criteria:* **Featured**, **Newest**, *or* **Recently Updated**.

Did You Know?

You can also search the WordPress Free Themes Directory (http:// wordpress.org/extend/themes) for themes. Most of these themes are also available from the Install Themes screen, however, with the advantage of automatic installation.

4 Click the **Find Themes** button at the bottom of the screen. WordPress displays thumbnails of all themes that match your criteria.

5 Click the **Preview** link to see a theme in more detail. This shows you a preview of the theme with the standard WordPress theme tester content. When you're finished previewing, click the **Close** button (x) in the upper-left corner of the preview window to close it and return to your list of matching themes.

6 Click the **Details** link to view more information about a theme, including its version number and user rating.

7 Click the **Install Now** link to install a theme on your site.

8 Click the **Live Preview** link to preview the theme with your own content. See "Using Live Preview" later in this chapter for more information.

9 Click the **Activate** link if you want to activate this theme now. (You can always activate later.)

When you activate a new theme, your previous theme is deactivated. Don't worry, though. WordPress doesn't delete the old theme (unless you do so manually), and you can reactivate it at any time.

Uploading a Theme (WordPress.org)

If you purchase a theme or download a free theme from the Web, you can install it directly from WordPress. Your theme must be in the .zip format to upload, which is the standard for packaging theme files.

Upload a Theme

① From the main navigation menu, select **Appearance**, **Themes**.

② Click the **Install Themes** tab.

③ Click the **Upload** link.

④ Click the **Browse** button.

5. Select the theme you want to upload in the File Upload dialog box, and click the **Open** button. Depending on your operating system and browser, the names of this dialog box and button might vary.

6. Click the **Install Now** button.

7. Click the **Live Preview** link to preview the theme with your own content. See "Using Live Preview" later in this chapter for more information.

8. Click the **Activate** link if you want to activate this theme now. (You can always activate later.)

Using Live Preview

Live Preview enables you to try out a new theme using the content from your own website. With Live Preview, you can also customize theme attributes including colors, header images, and more.

Preview a Theme with Live Preview

1. From the main navigation menu, select **Appearance, Themes**.

2. In the Available Themes section, click the **Live Preview** link below the theme you want to preview.

3. On the sidebar, make any changes to your theme. For example, you can change your site title and tagline, colors, header image, background image, or static front page (the options available vary by theme). WordPress displays any changes automatically in the preview window.

    IMPORTANT *With WordPress.com, the Live Preview sidebar is on the right, as shown in this example. With a self-hosted WordPress site, the sidebar is on the left.*

4. If you want to save your customization changes and activate this theme, click the **Save & Activate** button. WordPress saves any changes you made, activates the theme, and returns to the Manage Themes screen.

5. If you don't want to activate the theme or if you are not happy with your changes, click the **Cancel** button to return to the Manage Themes screen.

Activating a Different Theme

If you get tired of your site's current theme, you can activate another theme with the click of a button.

Activate a Different Theme

① From the main navigation menu, select **Appearance**, **Themes**.

> **IMPORTANT** *Activating a new theme can remove any customizations you made to your current theme (if you return to the old theme, WordPress remembers the customizations, however). If you made substantial customizations, be sure to back up your site first. If your site is new and you're just exploring themes, this isn't an issue.*

② In the Available Themes section, click the **Activate** link below the theme you want to activate.

See Also

See Chapter 18, "Managing Your WordPress Website," for more information about backups.

Did You Know?

If you use self-hosted WordPress, only themes you've installed display in the Available Themes section. You must first install a theme before you can activate it. On WordPress. com, no installation is necessary, and all themes are available from this section.

Customizing Your Theme

WordPress offers several options for customizing your theme, including the Theme Customizer, which enables you to customize your theme from an easy-to-use interface. In addition, some themes come with even more options you can customize on the Theme Options screen.

Customize Your Theme with the Theme Customizer

1 From the main navigation menu, select **Appearance**, **Themes**.

2 On the Manage Themes screen, click the **Customize** link below your active theme.

3 On the sidebar, make any changes to your theme. For example, you can change your site title and tagline, colors, header image, background image, or static front page (the options available vary by theme). WordPress displays any changes automatically in the preview window.

IMPORTANT *With WordPress.com, the Live Preview sidebar is on the right. With a self-hosted WordPress site, the sidebar is on the left, as shown in this example.*

4 When you're finished customizing, click the **Save & Publish** button. WordPress saves your changes and updates your website.

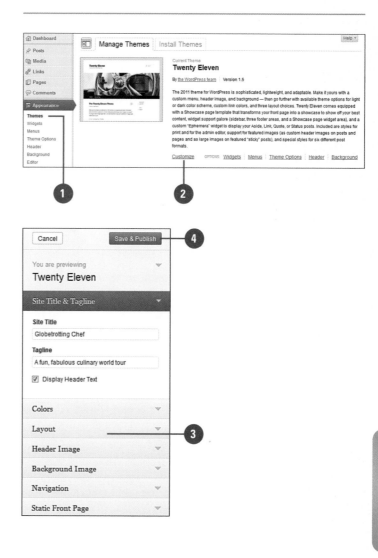

Customize Theme Options

1 From the main navigation menu, select **Appearance**, **Theme Options**.

> **TIMESAVER** *If you're already on the Manage Themes screen, click the **Theme Options** button below your active theme.*

2 Specify the options you want to change. The options that display on this screen vary by theme.

3 Click the **Save Options** button. WordPress saves your changes and applies them to your active theme.

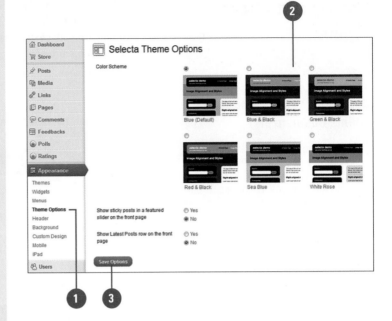

Add a Custom Header Image to Your Theme

IMPORTANT *The optimal size for your header image varies by theme. The Custom Header screen lets you know the best size for your current theme and displays a preview of your header.*

1. From the main navigation menu, select **Appearance, Header**.

2. If you want to upload a custom header image, click the **Browse** button.

TIMESAVER *If you already uploaded the image you want to use as your header, click the **Choose Image** button to select it from your WordPress media library.*

3. Select the image you want to upload in the File Upload dialog box, and click the **Open** button. Depending on your operating system and browser, the names of this dialog box and button might vary.

4. Click the **Upload** button.

Did You Know?

By default, WordPress displays the site title and tagline you entered on the General screen on your header. Optionally, you can use an image as your header, such as a logo.

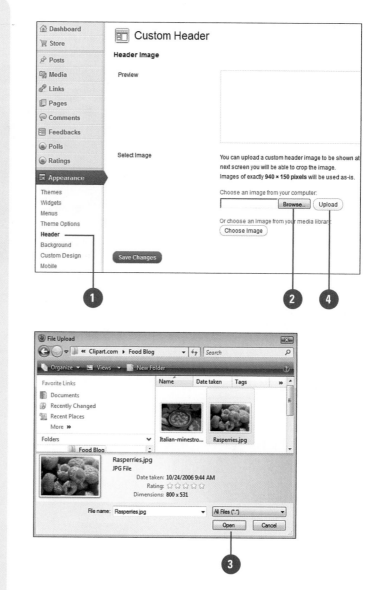

5 Select the part of the image you want to use as a header and click the **Crop and Publish** button.

6 Select the **Show Header Text with Your Image** check box if you want to display your site title and tagline with this image. This works best if your image doesn't contain any text.

7 Optionally, enter a **Text Color** if you chose to show header text. You can enter a color code (such as #006699) or click the **Select a Color** link to select a color from the palette. When selecting a color, aim for a shade that site visitors can read clearly when placed over your image.

8 Click the **Save Changes** button. WordPress displays a preview of your changes.

Did You Know?

In the preview, you can click the name of your site or the **Visit Your Site** link at the top of the screen to view your new header.

Did You Know?

If you don't like the header image you selected, click the **Remove Header Image** button to delete it.

TIMESAVER *You can also add a custom header image using the Theme Customizer. See "Customize Your Theme with the Theme Customizer" earlier in this chapter for more information.*

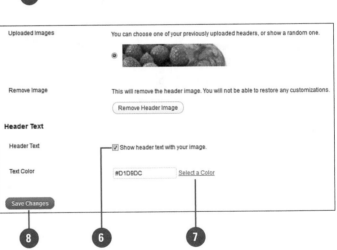

Customize Your Theme Background

1 From the main navigation menu, select **Appearance**, **Background**.

2 If you want to upload a custom background image, click the **Browse** button, select an image in the File Upload dialog box, and click the **Open** button.

TIMESAVER *If you already uploaded the image you want to use as your background, click the **Choose Image** button to select it from your WordPress media library.*

3 Click the **Upload** button. Word-Press displays a preview of your background.

Did You Know?

Most themes enable you to apply a custom background to your website. Although an attractive background can enhance your site, backgrounds don't work well with all themes. If you'd like to apply a background, try it out; you can always remove it with a single click.

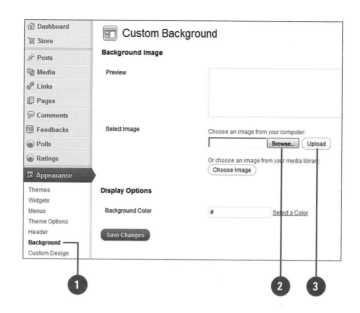

4 In the **Display Options** section, specify exactly how you want to display your background. For example, you can indicate its position, whether you want the image to repeat, or whether you want it to scroll or stay in a fixed location.

5 Click the **Save Changes** button. WordPress displays a preview of your changes.

Did You Know?

In the preview, you can click the name of your site or the **Visit Your Site** link at the top of the screen to view your new header.

Did You Know?

If your background image doesn't yield the desired results, click the **Remove Background Image** button to delete it.

TIMESAVER *You can also customize your theme background using the Theme Customizer. See "Customize Your Theme with the Theme Customizer" earlier in this chapter for more information.*

Remove Image

Remove Background Image
This will remove the background image. You will not be able to

Select Image

Choose an image from your computer:

Browse... Upload

Or choose an image from your media library:
Choose Image

Display Options

Position ● Left ○ Center ○ Right ———— **4**

Repeat ○ No Repeat ● Tile ○ Tile Horizontally ○ Tile Vertically

Attachment ● Scroll ○ Fixed

Background Color # Select a Color

Save Changes

5

Other Theme Customization Options (WordPress.org)

Although finding a theme that already meets most of your requirements saves you time and avoids potential customization headaches, you'll still probably want to change something about your theme. In addition to using the Theme Customizer, WordPress offers two other ways to customize your theme:

◆ **Use the options screens available for your active theme.** Many themes offer specialized customization options that help you tailor it to your specific needs. Although this is most common with premium themes, some free themes also offer theme options. To find these options, look for new selections on your main navigation menu on the left side of your screen. For example, Biznizz, a premium theme from Woo Themes, enables you to customize this theme's colors, fonts, and typography as well as add special theme layout options such as a slider, portfolio, scrolling testimonials, home page mini features, custom headers and footers, and much more.

◆ **Customize your theme CSS.** If you use WordPress.com, purchasing the Custom Design upgrade enables you to customize CSS beyond the limits of the Theme Customizer. If you use self-hosted WordPress, many themes offer a Custom CSS box or something similar where you can enter custom CSS that overrides the CSS on your themes stylesheet. If your theme doesn't offer this feature, the Jetpack plugin (http://wordpress.org/extend/plugins/jetpack/) includes a CSS editor.

Customization options for a premium theme

See Also

See Chapter 12, "Working with Plugins (WordPress.org)," for more information about installing and using plugins.

See Also

See Chapter 15, "Using WordPress.com Premium Features," for more information about the WordPress.com Custom Design upgrade, which lets you customize the fonts, colors, and CSS on your site.

Did You Know?

Although working with CSS is beyond the scope of this book, a good reference to check out is *Sams Teach Yourself HTML and CSS in 24 Hours* by Julie Meloni and Michael Morrison.

Deleting a Theme (WordPress.org)

If you no longer want a theme you installed, you can delete it.

Delete a Theme

1. From the main navigation menu, select **Appearance**, **Themes**.

2. In the Available Themes section, click the **Delete** link below the theme you want to delete.

3. In the warning dialog box that opens, click **OK**. WordPress deletes the theme.

IMPORTANT *Deleting isn't the same thing as simply deactivating one theme by activating another. When you delete a theme, it's no longer available on the Manage Themes screen, and you would need to install it again to activate it.*

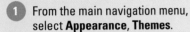

Creating and Managing Pages

Pages are an important part of your WordPress site, enabling you to create static content that's not part of your blog or feed. For example, pages for a business site might include About Us, Meet the Team, Clients, Products, Services, and Contact Us (you can probably get more creative with the names, though!). A blog might be a bit more informal, with pages to introduce and contact the blogger.

TIMESAVER *If you created a sitemap for your site, as recommended in Chapter 1, "Introducing WordPress," you should already know what pages and subpages your site needs and the content needed on each page. Using this plan, you can create all the pages for your site much faster.*

What You'll Do

Add Pages

Manage Pages

Copy Pages (WordPress.com)

Delete Pages

Adding Pages

In WordPress, you add a page on the Add New Page screen.

Add a Page

IMPORTANT *In this section, I describe the basic process for adding pages, but be aware that your own screen might have additional panels or options.*

1 From the main navigation menu, select **Pages**, **Add New**.

2 In the text box at the top of the screen, enter a descriptive title for your page.

3 Click the **Visual** tab, if it isn't already selected. The visual editor enables you to view your content as it will display on the Web, including any media and formatting you add.

4 Enter your page content in the large text box.

5 Format your text using the buttons on the menu bar. For example, you can apply bold or italic to selected text, add links, or create bullet lists.

6 If you want to insert a media file (such as an image, audio, or video), click the **Add Media** button and select your file in the Add Media dialog box.

7 Click the **Screen Options** button to display a pull-down tab of available screen options.

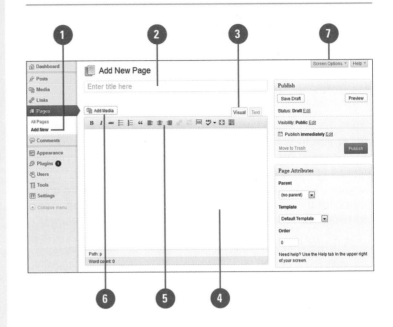

See Also

See Chapter 8, "Formatting Pages and Posts," for more information about formatting your pages.

For Your Information

Add New Page Panels

The panels that display on the Add New Page screen vary depending upon several things:

◆ Which version of WordPress you're using

◆ Your installed theme

◆ Your installed plugins (if using self-hosted WordPress)

◆ The screen options you select

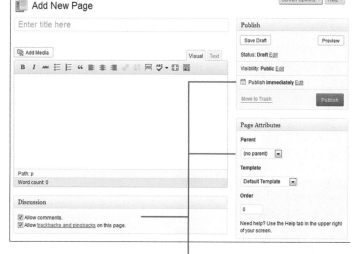

8. Select the panels you want to display on the Add New Page screen. Some panels display by default, whereas you need to activate others. See the sidebar "Displaying Panels on the Add New Page Screen" later in this chapter for more information about the available panels.

IMPORTANT *Explore the panels that come with your installed theme and plugins. These often provide added flexibility and functionality that enhance your site.*

9. Click the **Screen Options** button to close the pull-down tab.

TIMESAVER *WordPress saves the screen options you select for any future pages you add. If you've already specified screen options, you can skip steps 7–9.*

10. Enter any required information in the panels you added. For example, you might want to specify a parent page or select a template.

Did You Know?

If you know HTML, you can click the HTML tab and enter your page content in the HTML editor. This editor displays your page content as HTML code, which you can edit more precisely than visual content.

See Also

See Chapter 9, "Working with Media Files," for more information about adding media files.

11 By default, WordPress publishes your page immediately. If you want to schedule this page for publishing at a later date, click the **Edit** link next to the Publish field, select a date and time, and click **OK**. WordPress will publish this page at the date and time specified using the time zone you set up on the General Settings screen.

12 By default, WordPress makes your page public—visible to anyone on the Web. If you want to restrict visibility of this page, click the **Edit** link next to the Visibility field and select either **Password Protected** or **Private**.

13 WordPress creates a permalink for your page based on the page title. For example, a page titled "Healthcare Copywriting Services" would include the text "healthcare-copywriting-services" in its permalink. If you want to change the default text, click the **Edit** button and make your changes. One good reason for changing the default permalink is to shorten the link to a long page name.

14 Click the **Save Draft** button to save your page.

15 Click the **Preview** button to preview what your page will look like on the Web. If you're happy with what you see, continue to step 16. If not, make any changes before publishing.

16 If you're ready to publish your page, click the **Publish** button. If you're not ready to publish, you can publish at a later time. For example, many people save their pages as drafts and then publish after editing and review.

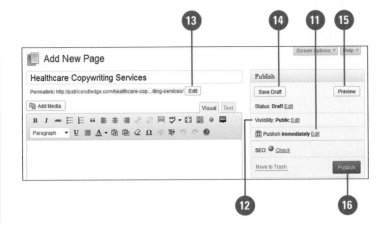

For Your Information

Password Protected Versus Private Pages

Selecting **Password Protected** enables you to enter a password for this page. Only users who know this password can access the page. A private post is visible only to the editors and admins on your WordPress site.

See Also

See "Specifying General Settings" in Chapter 4, "Specifying WordPress Settings," for more information about setting your time zone.

Displaying Panels on the Add New Page Screen

The Screen Options pull-down tab offers check boxes for the panels you can display on the Add New Page screen. Remember that some panels come with WordPress; others come with the themes or plugins you installed. For example, I use the Biznizz theme on one of my WordPress.org sites, which includes screen options for the Biznizz Custom Settings and Biznizz SEO Settings panels.

On this tab, you can also specify the number of columns you want to display on the Add New Page screen: one or two (the default).

If you use WordPress.com, this tab includes check boxes to show the feedback sidebar or to use Zemanta (www.zemanta.com) to find related content and images from around the Web (mostly useful for adding to your posts, but you could also use this for pages).

Here are some default panels that are particularly useful for pages:

- **Page Attributes**—The Page Attributes panel offers several important options. In this panel, you can
    - **Select a parent page if you want this page to be a subpage**—Subpages are useful for structuring your WordPress page content. For example, you could create a page to describe your services and then create subpages for each type of service.

- **Apply a page template**—Applying a template with a custom layout can be a real timesaver. The templates available from the Template drop-down list vary by theme. For example, you might find templates for a blog page, an image gallery, a portfolio, a contact form, or an archive page.

- **Specify the order of this page**—Specifying a page order lets WordPress know the order for displaying this page on your menu. Optionally, you can also control page menus on the Menus screen, which is covered in Chapter 13, "Adding and Managing Menus."

- **Discussion**—Specify whether you want to allow comments or trackbacks/pingbacks on this page. Many WordPress users prefer to allow comments on posts, but not on static pages.

- **Writing Helper** (WordPress.com)—The Writing Helper includes two sections: Copy a Page and Request Feedback. Copy a Page, as its name implies, enables you to copy an existing page as a starting point for your new page (see "Copy a Page" later in this chapter for more information). Request Feedback enables you to email selected people to ask for feedback on your page before posting. Optionally, you can also share a link with people without sending an email.

Managing Pages

On the Pages screen, you can view all your WordPress pages in one place. If you have only a few pages, it's easy to find the page you want. On the other hand, if your site contains numerous pages, WordPress offers several options for filtering, searching, and sorting pages to find exactly what you're looking for.

WordPress also makes it easy to edit your pages—both pages you saved as a draft and previously published pages. If you want to make some quick changes to a page's attributes without changing its content, you can use the Quick Edit feature.

View a Page

1 From the main navigation menu, select **Pages**.

2 By default, WordPress displays all your pages. Optionally, click the **Published** link to display only published pages.

3 To view only draft pages, click the **Drafts** link.

4 Click the **Title**, **Author**, or **Date** heading to sort your pages by one of these criteria.

5 If you want to filter your pages by date, select the month and year from the **Show All Dates** drop-down list and click the **Filter** button.

6 If you have a large number of pages, enter some text from the page you want to find in the text box in the upper-right corner and click the **Search Pages** button.

7 Click the title of a specific page you want to view.

Edit a Page

1. From the main navigation menu, select **Pages**.

2. On the Pages screen, pause your mouse over the page you want to edit and click the **Edit** link to open the Edit Page screen.

3. Make any changes to the page.

4. Click the **Preview Changes** button to preview your changes on the Web. If you're happy with what you see, continue to step 5. If not, you can make additional changes.

5. When you're finished, you can select from the following options in the Publish panel:

   ◆ Click the **Publish** button to publish a page you previously saved as a draft.

   ◆ Click the **Save Draft** button to update a page you previously saved as a draft.

   ◆ Click the **Update** button to update a page you previously published.

Perform a Quick Edit

1. From the main navigation menu, click **Pages**.

2. On the Pages screen, pause your mouse over the page you want to edit and click the **Quick Edit** link to open the Quick Edit section.

3. Make your changes to the page. For example, you can change a page title, change a page's status from Draft to Published, and so forth.

4. Click the **Update** button.

Copying Pages (WordPress.com)

Adding a new page to your site by copying an existing page is an easy way to save time.

Copy a Page

1. From the main navigation menu, select **Pages**, **Copy a Page**.

2. Optionally, enter some text from the title of the page you want to copy. WordPress displays only matching pages. This is particularly useful for sites that have numerous pages.

3. Click the **Copy** button to the left of the page you want to copy.

4. WordPress opens the Add New Page screen with a copy of the page you specified. From here, you can edit and publish your new page.

TIMESAVER *You can also copy a page by clicking the **Copy a Page** section in the Writing Helper panel on the Add New Page screen.*

IMPORTANT *The Writing Helper and its Copy a Page feature are available only in WordPress.com. To duplicate this functionality in WordPress.org, consider installing the Duplicate Post plugin (http:// wordpress.org/extend/plugins/ duplicate-post). Optionally, you can copy and paste page content to duplicate it. Be aware, however, that if your page contains links or embedded objects, copying and pasting from the HTML tab ensures that you don't lose any formatting.*

Deleting Pages

Deleting a WordPress page couldn't be easier; you can move pages to the Trash folder in a single click. Just in case you delete a page by mistake, however, WordPress lets you restore deleted pages and makes you confirm deletion before removing pages permanently from your site.

Delete a Page

① From the main navigation menu, select **Pages**.

② On the Pages screen, pause your mouse over the page you want to delete and click the **Trash** link below the page name. WordPress moves the page to the Trash folder.

> **TIMESAVER** *Do you want to delete multiple pages at once? Select the check box next to the pages you want to delete, select **Move to Trash** from the Bulk Actions drop-down list, and click the **Apply** button.*

> **IMPORTANT** *Did you delete a page by mistake? Click the **Undo** button at the top of the Pages screen to restore the page immediately. This button is available only when you first delete a page. If you want to restore a page later, you can do so from the Trash folder.*

Did You Know?

You can also delete a page by clicking the **Move to Trash** link in the Publish panel on the Add New Page screen or Edit Page screen.

Restore a Deleted Page

1. From the main navigation menu, select **Pages**.

2. On the Pages screen, click the **Trash** link at the top of the page.

3. Pause your mouse over the page you want to restore and click the **Restore** link. WordPress removes the page from the Trash folder and restores it to the Pages screen.

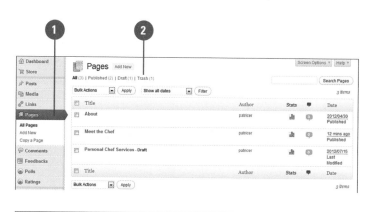

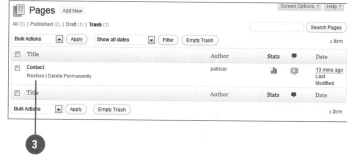

Empty Pages from the Trash Folder

1. From the main navigation menu, select **Pages**.

2. On the Pages screen, click the **Trash** link at the top of the page.

3. Click the **Empty Trash** button. WordPress deletes the selected pages permanently.

IMPORTANT *If you want to delete only one page permanently, pause your mouse over it and click the **Delete Permanently** link. Optionally, select the check boxes of multiple pages you want to empty from the Trash folder, select **Delete Permanently** from the Bulk Actions drop-down list, and click the **Apply** button.*

Creating and Managing Posts

Posts are the foundation of any blog—or the blog portion of a website. Although creating a post is very similar to creating a page, posts perform a different function on your site. On most sites, posts display on your home page (newest post first), or on a dedicated blog page. Your posts are also included in your site's feed, which readers can subscribe to.

IMPORTANT *If you're undecided whether to publish content as a post or a page, remember that a post provides greater visibility and encourages more interaction. Pages are best for static content such as information about you, your organization, and your contact details. Posts are best for everything else.*

TIMESAVER *If you created an editorial calendar for your site, as recommended in Chapter 1, "Introducing WordPress," you should already have a good idea about the posts you need to start off your site. Using this plan helps ensure you post new content on a regular basis and categorize it for maximum effectiveness.*

Did You Know?

Are you looking for even more options for creating posts? Check out the Press This bookmarklet (which enables you to clip content from the Web and post it on your site) or the Post via Email feature. See the section "Specifying Writing Settings" in Chapter 4, "Specifying WordPress Settings," to learn more about these options.

What You'll Do

Create a Post on the Add New Post Screen

Create a Post with QuickPress

Copy a Post (WordPress.com)

Create a Post Using the Quick Post Form (WordPress.com)

View All Posts

Edit and Delete Posts

Work with Categories

Work with Tags

Creating a Post on the Add New Post Screen

Creating posts on the Add New Post screen gives you the most control and flexibility over your posts' content and appearance.

The panels that display on this screen vary depending upon several things:

- Which version of WordPress you're using
- Your installed theme
- Your installed plugins (WordPress.org)
- The screen options you select

This task describes the basic process for creating posts, but be aware that your own screen might have additional panels or options.

Create a Post on the Add New Post Screen

1. From the main navigation menu, select **Posts**, **Add New**.

   TIMESAVER *Clicking the **New** button at the top of the screen is another way to open the Add New Post screen.*

2. In the text box at the top of the screen, enter a descriptive title for your post.

3. Click the **Visual** tab, if it isn't already selected. The visual editor enables you to view your content as it will display on the Web, including any media and formatting you add.

Click to add new post

Did You Know?

If you know HTML, you can click the Text tab and enter your post content in the HTML editor. This editor displays your post content as HTML code, which you can edit more precisely than visual content.

4 Enter your post content in the large text box.

5 Format your text using the buttons on the menu bar. For example, you can apply bold or italic to selected text, add links, or create bullet lists.

6 If you want to insert a media file (such as an image, audio, or video), click the **Add Media** button and select your file in the Insert Media dialog box.

7 In the upper-right corner of the screen, click the **Screen Options** button to display a pull-down tab of available screen options.

See Also

See Chapter 8, "Formatting Pages and Posts," for more information about formatting your posts.

See Also

See Chapter 9, "Working with Media Files," for more information about adding media files.

Add New Post

Screen Options ▼ Help ▼

Enter title here

Add Media   Visual | Text

B | I | ABC | ≣ ≣ | ≣ | " | ≣ ≣ ≣ | ⸜ ⸝ | ▦ ☺ ▼ | ⊡ | ▦

Publish

Save Draft   Preview

Status: **Draft** Edit

Visibility: **Public** Edit

📅 Publish **immediately** Edit

Move to Trash   Publish

For Your Information

Use Strategic Keywords in Your Post Titles and Content

When you create a post, your goal should be to create content that engages your readers while supporting your business goals. You also want your content to attract search engines (the best way to draw all those readers to your site).

For each post, think about the keywords readers would use to find this information. To determine how many people search for these keywords, use a tool such as the Google AdWords Keywords Tool (https://adwords.google.com/o/KeywordTool). Use your selected keywords in your title and in your post content several times. Be careful not to overdo keywords, however. Writing in a natural style that appeals to your readers is far more important than "stuffing" your content with keywords and hoping to rank well in search engines.

For example, suppose you want to write a post about infographics—specifically, software, tools, and templates for designing infographics. Your research tells you that although people do search for these keyword phrases, the related phrase "infographic design" is more popular than your original choices. Based on this information, you decide to call your post "Infographic Design: The Best Software, Tools, and Templates."

8 Select the panels you want to display on the Add New Post screen. Some panels display by default, whereas you need to activate others. See the sidebar "Displaying Panels on the Add New Post Screen" later in this chapter for more information about the available panels.

IMPORTANT *Explore the panels that come with your installed theme and plugins. These often provide added flexibility and functionality that enhance your site.*

9 Click the **Screen Options** button to close the pull-down tab.

TIMESAVER *WordPress saves the screen options you select for any future posts you add. If you've already specified screen options, you can skip steps 7–9.*

10 Enter any required information in the panels you added. For example, you might want to add tags, a featured image, or an excerpt.

11 Select a post format. By default, WordPress creates posts using the Standard format. The fields available in this panel vary based on your installed theme, but could include options for creating gallery, image, or quote posts, for example.

12 Select a category or categories for this post. If this is your first post and you haven't added any categories yet, click the **Add New Category** link to add a category and optional parent category; click the **Add New Category** button when you finish.

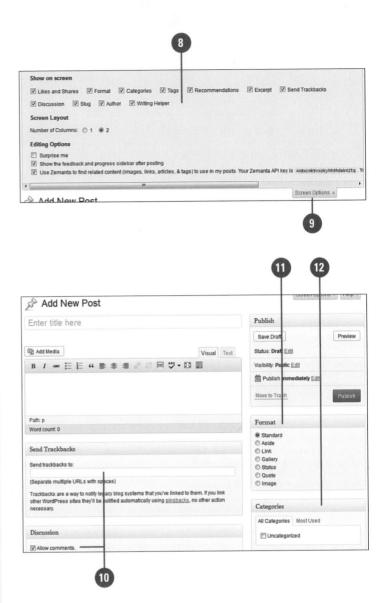

IMPORTANT *Can't find the Categories panel? Click the* **Screen Options** *button, select the* **Categories** *check box, and click the* **Screen Options** *button again to close the pull-down tab. See the "Displaying Panels on the Add New Post Screen" sidebar later in this chapter for more information.*

13 By default, WordPress publishes your post immediately. If you want to schedule this post for publishing at a later date, click the **Edit** link next to the Publish field, select a date and time, and click **OK**. WordPress will publish this post at the date and time specified using the time zone you set up on the General Settings screen.

14 By default, WordPress sets the visibility to Public, which means the post is visible to anyone on the Web. If you want to restrict visibility of this post, click the **Edit** link next to the Visibility field and select either **Password Protected** or **Private**.

See Also

See "Working with Categories" later in this chapter to learn more about post categories.

For Your Information

Password Protected Versus Private Posts

Selecting **Password Protected** enables you to enter a password for this post. Only users who know this password can access the post. Selecting **Private** makes a post visible only to the editors and admins on your WordPress site.

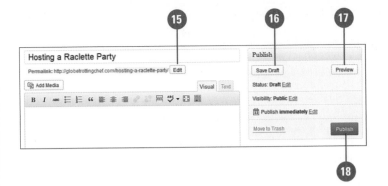

15 WordPress creates a permalink for your post based on the post title. For example a post titled "Hosting a Raclette Party" would include the text "hosting-a-raclette-party" in its permalink. If you want to change the default text, click the **Edit** button and make your changes. One good reason for changing the default permalink is to shorten the link for a long post name.

16 Click the **Save Draft** button to save your post.

17 Click the **Preview** button to see what your post will look like on the Web. If you're happy with the post, continue to step 18. If not, make any changes before publishing.

18 If you're ready to publish your post, click the **Publish** button. If you're not ready to publish, you can publish at a later time. For example, many people save their posts as drafts and then publish after editing and reviewing.

See Also

See the section "Specifying General Settings" in Chapter 4 for more information about specifying your time zone.

See Also

See the section "Customizing Permalinks Settings" in Chapter 4 for more information about the different ways you can format your site's permalinks.

Displaying Panels on the Add New Post Screen

The Screen Options pull-down tab offers check boxes for the panels you can display on the Add New Post screen. Remember that some panels come with WordPress; others come with the theme or plugins you installed. For example, I use the Biznizz theme on one of my WordPress.org sites, which includes screen options for the Biznizz Custom Settings and Biznizz SEO Settings panels.

On this tab, you can also specify the number of columns you want to display on the Add New Post screen: one or two (the default).

Here are some default panels that are particu-
posts:

—Specify one or more catego-
gn to your post. Categories are
l part of organizing your post
d you should assign each post
one category. See "Working with
" later in this chapter for more
n.

- **Tags**—Enter tags to identify the topics covered in a post. See "Working with Tags" later in this chapter for more information.

- **Excerpt**—Enter a brief excerpt or summary of your post. Many WordPress themes display post summaries on your site's home page or on a category page.

- **Send Trackbacks**—Enter the URL of a post on a non-WordPress site you mention in your post. For example, suppose you read a great post on the Dining in Denver blog. You mention this post on your own food blog, enter the URL of the original post in the Send Trackbacks panel, and WordPress displays this as a comment on the original

post. If you mention a post on another WordPress site, WordPress handles notifications automatically via pingbacks.

- **Discussion**—Specify whether you want to allow comments, pingbacks, or trackbacks on this post. Many WordPress users prefer to allow comments on posts, but not on static pages.

- **Author**—Identify the post author on a multi-author site.

- **Format**—Select a format for your post from the available options. Post formats are theme-specific are could include options such as Standard, Aside, Image, or Gallery.

- **Writing Helper** (WordPress.com)—Display the Writing Helper, which includes two sections: Copy a Post and Request Feedback. Copy a Post, as its name implies, enables you to copy an existing post as a starting point for your new post (see "Copying a Post (WordPress.com)" later in this chapter for more information). Request Feedback enables you to email selected people to ask for feedback on your post before posting. Optionally, you can also share a link with people without sending an email.

- **Likes and Shares** (WordPress.com)—Display likes and sharing buttons on selected posts.

- **Recommendations** (WordPress.com)—Insert images and content from around the Web into your posts via Zemanta (www.zemanta.com).

Creating a Post with QuickPress

If you want to create a basic post quickly, consider using the Quick-Press box on your WordPress Dashboard. Because QuickPress doesn't let you assign a category or format text, it's most useful for creating quick drafts, but you can publish from QuickPress if you want.

Create a Post with QuickPress

1. If your WordPress Dashboard isn't already open, click **Dashboard** on the main navigation menu.

2. In the QuickPress section, enter a descriptive title for your post in the text box.

3. In the Content box, enter your post content.

4. If you want to insert a media file (such as an image, audio, or video), click the **Add Media** button and select your file in the Insert Media dialog box.

5. Optionally, enter tags that identify the topic of your post in the **Tags** field.

6. If you want to save this post as a draft for later editing and publishing, click the **Save Draft** button.

7. If you want to publish your post now, click the **Publish** button.

> **TIMESAVER** *Do you want to clear out the content you entered and start over? Click the **Reset** button.*

Did You Know?

If you're new to WordPress, the Welcome to Your WordPress Site! screen might display. If so, click the **Dismiss** link in the upper-right corner to close this screen and open the Dashboard.

Did You Know?

If you're using WordPress.com, the Add Poll button and Add a Custom Form button display next to the Add Media button. See Chapter 14, "Getting Feedback on Your Website (WordPress.com)," for more information.

See Also

See Chapter 9 for more information about adding media files.

Copying a Post (WordPress.com)

Adding a new post to your site by copying an existing post is an easy way to save time.

Copy a Post (WordPress.com)

1 From the main navigation menu, select **Posts**, **Copy a Post**.

2 Optionally, enter some text from the title of the post you want to copy. WordPress displays only matching posts. This is particularly useful for sites that have numerous posts.

3 Click the **Copy** button to the left of the post you want to copy.

4 WordPress opens the Add New Post screen with a copy of the post you specified. From here, you can edit and publish your new post.

TIMESAVER *You can also copy a post by clicking the Copy a Post section in the Writing Helper panel on the Add New Post screen.*

IMPORTANT *The Writing Helper and its Copy a Post feature are available only in WordPress.com. To duplicate this functionality in WordPress.org, consider installing the Duplicate Post plugin (http://wordpress.org/extend/plugins/duplicate-post). Optionally, you can copy and paste post content to duplicate it. Be aware, however, that if your post contains links or embedded objects, copying and pasting from the Text tab ensures that you don't lose any formatting.*

Creating a Post Using the Quick Post Form (WordPress.com)

Yet another option for creating a post is the Quick Post form on the WordPress.com home page.

Create a Post Using the Quick Post Form (Wordpress.com)

1. Navigate to www.wordpress.com while logged in to your WordPress account.

   TIMESAVER *You can also access this feature by clicking the* **Try It Now** *link in the QuickPress section on your Dashboard.*

2. Click the **New Post** button.

3. If you have more than one Word-Press.com site, select the site to post to from the drop-down list.

4. Click the button that represents the type of post you want to create: Text, Photo, Video, Quote, or Link. In this example, you create a Text post.

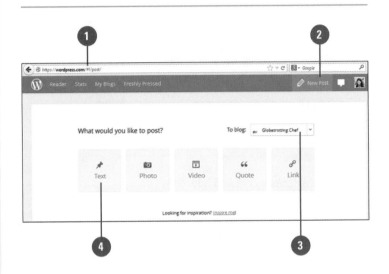

5 Enter a descriptive title for your post in the **Title** field.

6 Enter your content in the large text box.

7 Format your text using the buttons on the menu bar. For example, you can apply bold or italic to selected text, add links, or create bullet lists.

8 If you want to insert a photo, click the **Insert Photo** button, select the photo in the File Upload dialog box, and click the **Open** button. The names of this dialog box and button might vary depending on your operating system and browser.

9 Optionally, enter a list of post tags separated by commas.

10 Click the **Save Draft** button to save your post as a draft. (You can publish at a later date.)

11 Click the **Preview** button to preview your post in a browser.

12 Click the **Publish Post** button to post on your site.

See Also

See Chapter 8 for more information about formatting your posts.

Viewing All Posts

On the Posts screen, you can view all your WordPress posts in one place. If you have only a few posts, it's easy to find the post you want. On the other hand, if your site contains numerous posts, WordPress offers several options for filtering, searching, and sorting posts to find exactly what you're looking for.

View All Posts

1. From the main navigation menu, select **Posts**.

2. By default, WordPress displays all your posts. Optionally, click the **Published** link to display only published posts.

3. To view only draft posts, click the **Drafts** link.

4. Click the **Title**, **Author**, or **Date** heading to sort your posts by this criteria.

5. If you want to filter your posts by date, select the month and year from the **Show All Dates** drop-down list and click the **Filter** button.

6. If you want to filter your posts by category, select the category from the **View All Categories** drop-down list and click the **Filter** button.

7. To view excerpts of your posts, click the **Excerpt View** icon. To return to the default view, click the **List View** icon.

8. If you have a large number of posts, enter some text from the post you want to find in the text box in the upper-right corner and click the **Search Posts** button.

9. Click the title of a specific post you want to view.

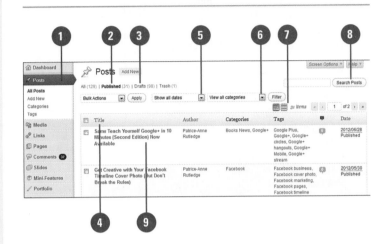

Editing and Deleting Posts

WordPress makes it easy to edit your posts, both posts you saved as a draft and previously published posts. If you want to make some quick changes to a post's attributes without changing its content, you can use the Quick Edit feature.

Deleting a WordPress post couldn't be easier; you can move posts to the Trash folder in a single click. In case you delete by mistake, WordPress lets you restore deleted posts. As an extra precaution, WordPress makes you confirm a deletion before removing posts permanently from your site.

Edit a Post

1. From the main navigation menu, select **Posts**.

2. On the Posts screen, pause your mouse over the post you want to edit and click the **Edit** link to open the Edit Post screen.

3. Make any changes to the post.

4. Click the **Preview** button to see how your changes will look on the Web. If you're happy with what you see, continue to step 5. If not, you can make additional changes.

5. When you're finished, you can select from the following options in the Publish panel:

   ◆ Click the **Publish** button to publish a post you previously saved as a draft.

   ◆ Click the **Save Draft** button to update a post you previously saved as a draft.

   ◆ Click the **Update** button to update a post you previously published.

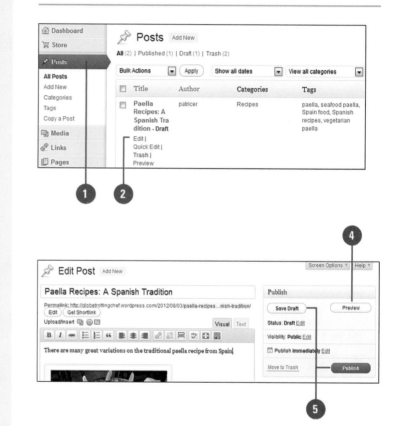

Perform a Quick Edit

1 From the main navigation menu, select **Posts**.

2 On the Posts screen, pause your mouse over the post you want to edit and click the **Quick Edit** link to open the Quick Edit section.

3 Make your changes to the post. For example, you can change a post's title, category, status, and so forth.

4 Click the **Update** button.

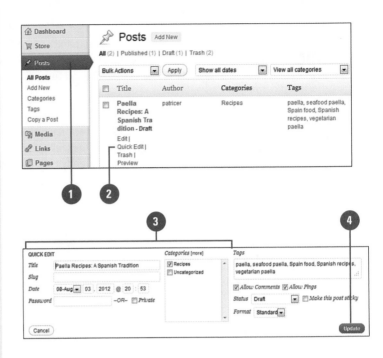

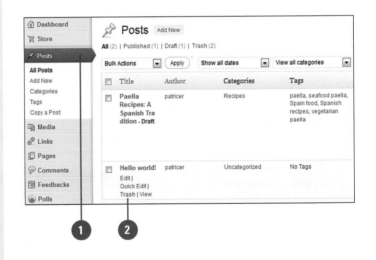

Delete a Post

1 From the main navigation menu, select **Posts**.

2 On the Posts screen, pause your mouse over the post you want to delete and click the **Trash** link below the post name. WordPress moves the post to the Trash folder.

TIMESAVER *Do you want to delete multiple posts at once? Select the check box next to the posts you want to delete, select **Move to Trash** from the Bulk Actions drop-down list, and click the **Apply** button.*

IMPORTANT *Did you delete a post by mistake? Click the **Undo** button at the top of the Posts screen to restore the post immediately. This button is available only when you first delete a post. If you want to restore a post later, you can do so from the Trash folder.*

Did You Know?

You can also delete a post by clicking the **Move to Trash** link in the Publish panel on the Add New Post screen or Edit Post screen.

Restore a Deleted Post

① From the main navigation menu, select **Posts**.

② On the Posts screen, click the **Trash** link at the top of the post.

③ Pause your mouse over the post you want to restore and click the **Restore** link. WordPress removes the post from the Trash folder and restores it to the Posts screen.

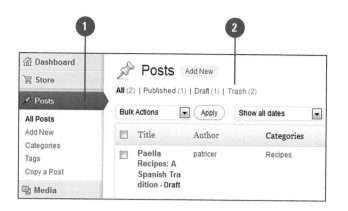

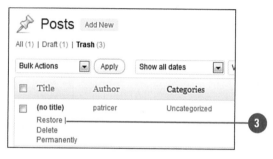

Empty Posts from the Trash Folder

① From the main navigation menu, select **Posts**.

② On the Posts screen, click the **Trash** link at the top of the post.

③ Click the **Empty Trash** button. Word-Press deletes the selected posts permanently.

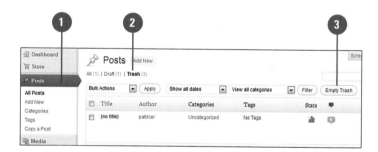

> **IMPORTANT** *If you want to delete only one post permanently, pause your mouse over it and click the **Delete Permanently** link. Optionally, select the check boxes of multiple posts you want to empty from the Trash folder, select **Delete Permanently** from the Bulk Actions drop-down list, and click the **Apply** button.*

Working with Categories

When you first create your site, think about the post categories you'll need. Although you can always add or delete categories later, it's a good idea to start with some basic categories to organize your posts.

Although you can add a new category when you create a post on the Add New Post screen, you can also add categories on the Categories screen. If you want to add multiple categories, doing so here will save you time. After you create your categories, you can view, manage, edit, or delete them on the Categories screen.

Add a New Category

1. From the main navigation menu, select **Posts**, **Categories**.

2. Enter a category name in the **Name** field.

3. (WordPress.org) Enter a category **Slug**. The slug displays at the end of the URL for that category and should be lowercase with only letters, numbers, and hyphens.

4. If this category is a subcategory, select its parent category from the **Parent** drop-down list. For example, a Social Media category could have subcategories for individual social sites, such as LinkedIn, Facebook, and so forth.

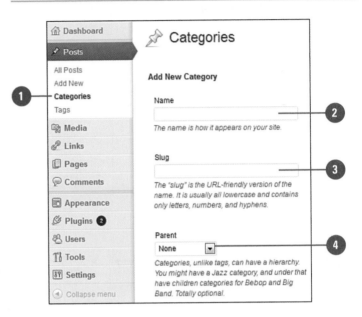

See Also

See "Planning Your Site" in Chapter 1 for more information about planning for the categories your site needs.

For Your Information

Categories Versus Tags

In WordPress, you use categories to define broad groups of posts. In general, you should aim for 10 or fewer categories. Tags, however, describe your posts in more detail. Keywords often make good tags, for example. See the section "Working with Tags" later in this chapter for more information about tags.

⑤ Optionally, enter a category **Description**. Some themes display this description, but not all do.

⑥ Click the **Add New Category** button. WordPress displays your new category in the panel on the right side of the screen.

View All Categories

① From the main navigation menu, select **Posts**, **Categories**.

② Click the **Name**, **Description**, **Slug**, or (number of) **Posts** heading to sort categories by this criteria.

③ If you have a large number of categories, enter some text from the category you want to find in the text box in the upper-right corner and click the **Search Categories** button.

④ To view all the posts associated with a specific category, pause your mouse over that category and click the **View** link. WordPress displays all posts for that category.

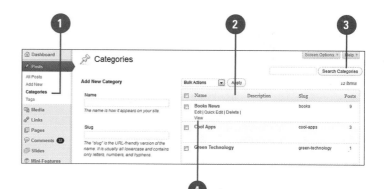

Edit a Category

1. From the main navigation menu, select **Posts**, **Categories**.

2. On the Categories screen, pause your mouse over the category you want to edit and click the **Edit** link. The Edit Category screen opens.

   TIMESAVER *If you just want to change the category name or slug, click the **Quick Edit** link on the Category screen, make your changes, and click the **Update Category** button.*

3. On the Edit Category screen, make any changes to the link category, including the name, slug, parent, or description.

   IMPORTANT *Changing a category name or slug doesn't remove the category from associated posts. WordPress simply updates the posts to the new name or slug.*

4. Click the **Update** button to save your changes.

Delete a Category

IMPORTANT *If you delete a category with assigned posts, WordPress transfers these posts to the Uncategorized category.*

1. From the main navigation menu, select **Posts**, **Categories**.

2. On the Categories screen, pause your mouse over the category you want to delete and click the **Delete** link below its name. WordPress deletes the category permanently.

3. Click **OK** to delete the category permanently.

IMPORTANT *You can't delete your default category, which Word-Press defines as Uncategorized. If you want to delete Uncategorized, you must first assign another category as default on the Writing Settings screen.*

TIMESAVER *To delete multiple categories at the same time, select the check box next to the categories you want to delete, select **Delete** from the Bulk Actions drop-down list, and click the **Apply** button.*

Working with Tags

Tags offer another way to identify the topics covered in a post. Whereas a category identifies the general focus of the post, tags can take this a step further. For example, you could assign a post about your trip to San Francisco to the Travel category and then apply the following tags: San Francisco, Golden Gate Bridge, North Beach, and cable cars. Tags are an optional, but useful, WordPress feature.

You'll probably add most of your tags directly on the Add New Post screen when you create a post, but you can also do so on the Tags screen, where you can also view, manage, edit, and delete tags.

Add a New Tag

① From the main navigation menu, select **Posts**, **Tags**.

② On the Tags screen, enter a tag name in the **Name** field.

③ (WordPress.org) Enter a tag **Slug**. The slug displays at the end of the URL for that tag and should be lowercase with only letters, numbers, and hyphens.

④ Optionally, enter a tag **Description**. Some themes display this description, but not all do.

⑤ Click the **Add New Tag** button. WordPress displays your new tag in the panel on the right side of the screen.

View All Tags

1. From the main navigation menu, select **Posts**, **Tags**.

2. Click the **Name**, **Description**, **Slug**, or (number of) **Posts** heading to sort tags by this criteria.

3. If you have a large number of tags, enter some text from the tag you want to find in the text box in the upper-right corner and click the **Search Tags** button.

4. To view all the posts associated with a specific tag, pause your mouse over that tag and click the **View** link.

5. View a list of popular tags you've used with your posts.

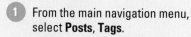

Edit a Tag

① From the main navigation menu, select **Posts**, **Tags**.

② On the Tags screen, pause your mouse over the tag you want to edit and click the **Edit** link. The Edit Tag screen opens.

IMPORTANT *Changing a tag name or slug doesn't remove the tag from associated posts. WordPress simply updates the posts to the new name or slug.*

TIMESAVER *If you just want to change the tag name or slug, click the **Quick Edit** link, make your changes, and click the **Update Tag** button—directly on the Tags screen.*

③ On the Edit Tag screen, make any changes to the tag, including the name, slug, or description.

④ Click the **Update** button to save your changes.

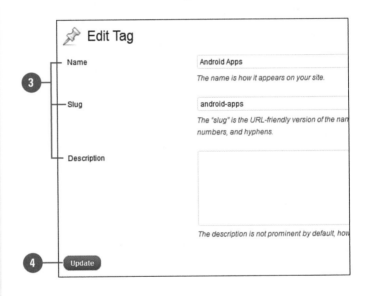

Delete a Tag

① From the main navigation menu, select **Posts**, **Tags**.

② On the Tags screen, pause your mouse over the tag you want to delete and click the **Delete** link below its name. WordPress deletes the tag permanently.

③ Click **OK** to delete the tag permanently.

TIMESAVER *To delete multiple tags at the same time, select the check box next to the tags you want to delete, select **Delete** from the Bulk Actions drop-down list, and click the **Apply** button.*

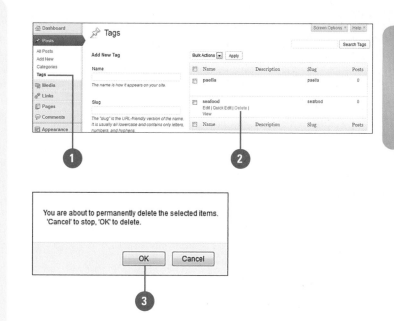

Formatting Pages and Posts

WordPress makes it easy to precisely format the content you enter on your website's pages and posts. In addition to traditional formatting options, such as adding bold and italic to text, creating lists, inserting links, and checking spelling, WordPress also offers several advanced formatting features.

You can use the More tag, for example, to break up long posts for enhanced readability on your home page and archive pages. The Distraction Free Writing mode provides a blank screen for writing without numerous menus, buttons, and other options to distract you from creating content. Finally, if you have knowledge of HTML, you can edit the code on your pages and posts.

WordPress offers two editing modes you can use to edit and format your content:

◆ **Visual Editor**—This is the default editing mode and enables you to enter and format content using a view that's similar to a word processing application, such as Microsoft Word.

◆ **Text Editor**—With the Text Editor, you can edit your content's HTML.

Formatting with the Visual Editor

The Visual Editor offers a WYSIWYG (What You See Is What You Get) editing environment with two rows of toolbar buttons above your content. If you use Microsoft Word or another word processing application, this type of content editor should be very familiar to you. The Visual Editor is the default WordPress editor, but if you switch to the Text Editor, you can return to the Visual Editor by clicking the Visual tab.

Toolbar   Visual tab

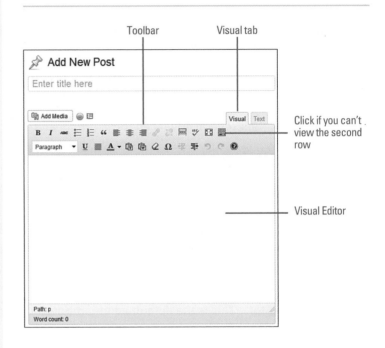

Click if you can't view the second row

Visual Editor

Exploring the Visual Editor Toolbar

Before you start editing content with the Visual Editor, you should take a few minutes to review the buttons on its toolbar. WordPress comes with a standard set of toolbar buttons, but some plugins or themes add new toolbar buttons for you to use.

Visual Editor Toolbar Buttons

Button	Description
Top Row	
Bold (Ctrl+B)	Add bold to the selected text.
Italic (Ctrl+I)	Add italic to the selected text.
Strikethrough (Alt+Shift+D)	Draw a line through the selected text.
Unordered List (Alt+Shift+U)	Apply bullets to the selected text.
Ordered List (Alt+Shift+O)	Apply automatic numbering to the selected text.
Blockquote (Alt+Shift+Q)	Highlight selected text as a quote. Your active theme determines the appearance and formatting of a blockquote.
Align Left (Alt+Shift+L)	Align text to the object's left margin.
Align Center (Alt+Shift+C)	Center text within the object.
Align Right (Alt+Shift+R)	Align text to the object's right margin.
Insert/Edit Link (Alt+Shift+A)	Insert or edit a hyperlink to an external site or another page or post on your website.
Unlink (Alt+Shift+S)	Remove a link you applied.
Insert More Tag (Alt+Shift+T)	Split long blog posts to display only certain text on your home page and archive pages. Available only for posts, not pages.
Proofread Writing (WordPress.com); Toggle Spellchecker (WordPress.org)	Check spelling, grammar, and style.
Distraction Free Writing Mode (Alt+Shift+W)	Open a minimalist view that displays only your content and a basic toolbar.
Show/Hide Kitchen Sink (Alt+Shift+Z)	Show or hide the bottom row of icons.

continues

Button	Description
Bottom Row	
Style	Apply a style from the drop-down list to selected text, such as a heading (H1, H2, and so forth) or a style defined by your theme.
Underline	Place a line under the selected text.
Align Full (Alt+Shift+J)	Space words and letters within words so that text touches both margins in the object.
Select Text Color	Click the icon directly to apply the current color to selected text. To choose another color, click the down arrow and select from the palette or color picker.
Paste as Plain Text	Open the Paste as Plain Text dialog box, where you can paste existing text into WordPress (using Ctrl+C to copy and Ctrl+V to paste) without adding any unwanted formatting.
Paste from Word	Open the Paste as Plain Text dialog box, where you can paste existing Microsoft Word content into WordPress (using Ctrl+C to copy and Ctrl+V to paste) without adding any unwanted formatting from Word.
Remove Formatting	Clear all formatting from selected text, such as bold, italic, color, underline, and so forth.
Insert Custom Character	Open the Select Custom Character dialog box where you can select a symbol to insert, such as an em dash, bullet, or accented character.
Outdent	Move the selected text to the left.
Indent	Move the selected text to the right.
Undo (Ctrl+Z)	Undo the previous action.
Redo (Ctrl+V)	Redo the previous action.
Help (Alt+Shift+H)	Open a help window with tips on using the editor as well as a list of hotkeys.

TIMESAVER *Pause your mouse over each toolbar button to display its description.*

IMPORTANT *Can't see the second toolbar row? Click the* **Show/Hide Kitchen Sink** *button to display it.*

TIMESAVER *Many of the buttons on the Visual tab have keyboard shortcuts, such as pressing Ctrl+B to bold selected text. The table in this section lists the corresponding shortcut if one is available.*

Creating a List

WordPress enables you to create two kinds of lists: unordered (bullet) and ordered (numbered).

Create a List

1. Open the page or post in which you want to create a list.

2. In the Visual Editor, select the text you want to format as a list.

3. Click the **Unordered List** button (or press Alt+Shift+U) to create a bulleted list.

4. Click the **Ordered List** button (or press Alt+Shift+O) to create a numbered list.

Did You Know?

Remember that you can open or create pages and posts using the options on the Pages and Posts menus on the left side of your screen.

Creating a Blockquote

Applying a blockquote to selected text is a great way to make it stand out. Your active theme controls the formatting and appearance of blockquotes.

Create a Blockquote

1. Open the page or post in which you want to create a blockquote.

2. In the Visual Editor, select the text you want to format as a blockquote.

3. Click the **Blockquote** button (or press Alt+Shift+Q).

Did You Know?

You can remove the blockquote formatting from the text by selecting it and clicking the **Blockquote** button again.

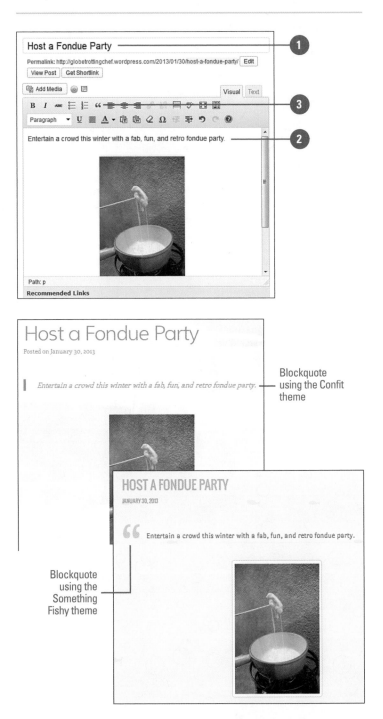

Blockquote using the Confit theme

Blockquote using the Something Fishy theme

Working with Links

Linking to other content is an important part of creating a high-quality, useful website. With WordPress, you can add links to external websites or to other pages and posts on your own website. You can add a link to selected text or an image.

Insert a Link

1. Open the page or post where you want to add a link.

2. In the Visual Editor, select the text or image to which you want to add a link.

3. Click the **Insert/Edit Link** button (or press Alt+Shift+A).

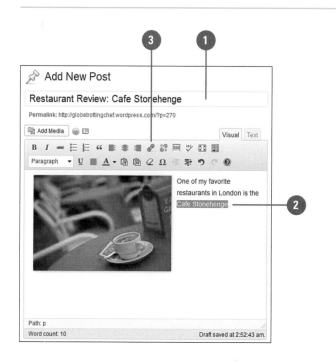

④ In the Insert/Edit Link dialog box, enter the **URL** to which you want to link.

TIMESAVER *Copy and paste the URL you want from your browser to save time and ensure accuracy.*

⑤ Enter a **Title** for your link.

⑥ If you want the linked page to open in a new window, select the **Open Link in a New Window/Tab** check box.

⑦ If you want to create an internal link within your website, click the **Or to Existing Content** section and select one of your site's pages or posts from the list.

TIMESAVER *If your site contains a lot of content, you can search for the page or post title you want in the Search box.*

⑧ Click **Add Link**.

⑨ WordPress adds the link. If you added a link to text, WordPress underlines it.

IMPORTANT *Test your link before publishing to ensure that it works correctly by previewing the page or post where you inserted it.*

Did You Know?

Opening an external page in a new window helps keep readers on your site.

Edit a Link

1. Open the page or post that contains the link you want to edit.

2. In the Visual Editor, select the linked text or image.

3. Click the **Insert/Edit Link** button (or press Alt+Shift+A).

4. Make your changes in the Insert/Edit Link dialog box.

5. Click the **Update** button.

Delete a Link

1. Open the page or post that contains the link you want to remove.

2. In the Visual Editor, select the linked text or image.

3. Click the **Unlink** button (or press Alt+Shift+S).

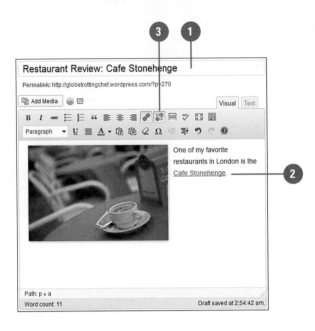

Using the More Tag

If you have a long blog post, you should consider using the More tag to split your post. This way only the initial text (such as the first paragraph) displays on your home page or archive pages. When you use the More tag, WordPress displays a link that readers can click to continue reading the post.

Add the More Tag to a Post

1. From the main navigation menu, select **Posts, Add New**.

2. In the Visual Editor, begin entering your new post.

3. When you reach the point where you want to split your content, click the **Insert More Tag** button (or press Alt+Shift+T).

   IMPORTANT *The More tag is available only for posts. It wouldn't make sense to split a page, because only posts display in sequence on your home page or archive pages.*

4. WordPress displays the More tag in your post.

5. Continue writing your post.

6. Click the **Publish** button when you're ready to publish your post.

7. WordPress displays the truncated post on your home page and archive pages.

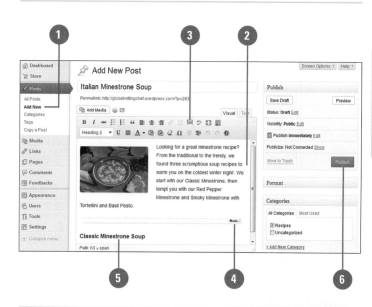

Customizing More Tag Links

Want to customize the link text that WordPress uses to encourage people to continue reading? Click the **Text** tab, look for the <!--more--> tag, add a space after the word "more," and enter your desired text. For example, you could replace the standard text with text that better reflects your brand, uses targeted keywords, or offers a call to action such as <!--more View our three favorite minestrone recipes-->.

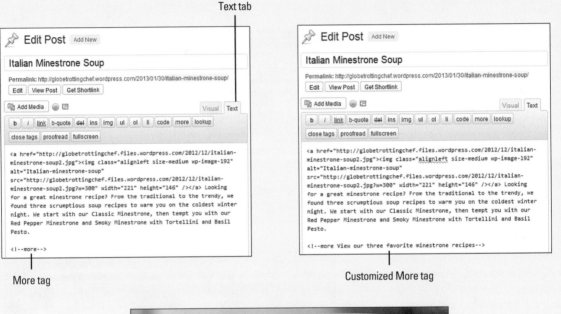

Text tab

More tag

Customized More tag

Customized link in browser

Checking Spelling, Grammar, and Style

Ensuring that your website content is grammatically correct and free of typographical errors is critical to its success. Fortunately, WordPress uses After the Deadline proofreading technology (http://www.afterthedeadline.com) to help you create quality content.

Check Spelling, Grammar, and Style

1. Open the page or post you want to proofread.

2. In the Visual Editor, click the **Proofread Writing** button.

3. WordPress underlines potential spelling errors in red, grammar errors in green, and style errors in blue.

4. Click a suspected error to view suggested corrections.

> **TIMESAVER** *You can set up default proofreading settings on the Personal Settings screen in Word-Press.com (select **Users**, **Personal Settings** from the menu) or the Profile screen for self-hosted WordPress (select **Users**, **Your Profile**). For example, you can select the grammar rules you want Word-Press to follow, specify whether you want WordPress to proofread content automatically, and more. See Chapter 16, "Managing Users," for more information.*

> **IMPORTANT** *Although After the Deadline does a good job of finding common typos, it can also flag words that aren't really errors. Using an automated tool can help catch some mistakes, but it doesn't take the place of a thorough proof-reading by a real person.*

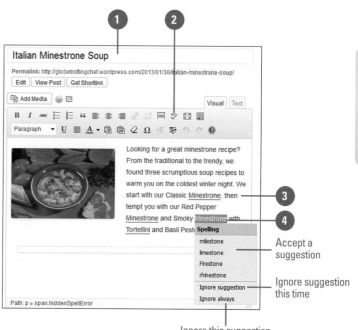

Accept a suggestion

Ignore suggestion this time

Ignore this suggestion always (not an error)

Using the Distraction Free Writing Mode

If you want to focus specifically on writing website content without the distraction of WordPress menus, buttons, and options, you can use Distraction Free Writing mode. This mode opens a minimalist view that displays only your content and a basic toolbar.

Use the Distraction Free Writing Mode

1. Open the page or post for which you want to use the Distraction Free Writing mode.

2. In the Visual Editor, click the **Distraction Free Writing Mode** button (or press Alt+Shift+W).

3. Enter your content in the text box.

4. Click **Save** to save your content. (Click **Update** if you've already published and are just making changes).

   IMPORTANT *To view the toolbar, buttons, or links in Distraction Free Writing mode, move your mouse to the top of the screen. These elements disappear again after a few seconds of inactivity.*

5. Click the **Exit Fullscreen** link to return to the regular WordPress view.

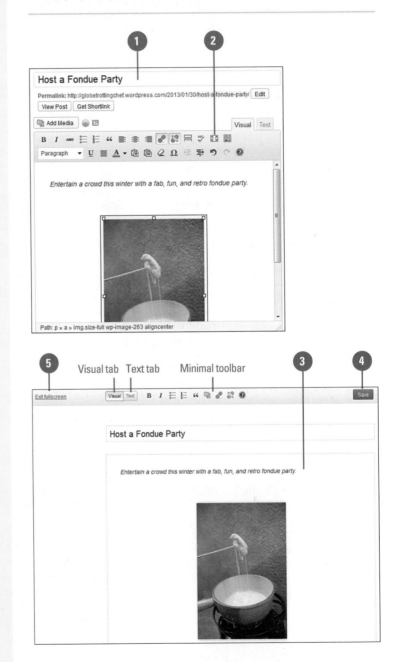

Formatting with the Text Editor

The Text Editor enables you to edit your pages and posts using Hypertext Markup Language (HTML), a popular markup language for the Web. Although you can create a quality website without editing any HTML, learning some basic HTML helps you expand your WordPress skills and enables you to make more advanced customizations.

Format with the Text Editor

1. Open the page or post you want to edit using the Text Editor.

2. Click the **Text** tab.

3. Edit your content directly in the Text Editor.

> **IMPORTANT** *Use caution when making changes in the Text Editor, particularly if your HTML skills are limited. Accidentally removing a required tag or other element can cause major formatting issues.*

Did You Know?

Providing a detailed HTML tutorial is beyond the scope of this book. The w3schools.com website offers an HTML tutorial at http://www.w3schools.com/html/default.asp and a list of HTML tags at http://www.w3schools.com/tags/default.asp. If you want a more in-depth HTML guide, check out *HTML5 & CSS3 Visual QuickStart Guide, 7th Edition* (Peachpit Press) by Elizabeth Castro and Bruce Hyslop.

Toolbar buttons

Exploring the Text Editor Toolbar

Before you start editing content with the Text Editor, you should take a few minutes to review the buttons on its toolbar. Most of these buttons correspond to HTML tags, but a few are specific to WordPress.

Text Editor Toolbar Buttons

Button	Description
B	Add bold to the selected text.
I	Add italic to the selected text.
Link	Insert or edit a hyperlink to an external site or another page or post on your website.
b-quote	Highlight selected text as a quote. Your active theme determines the appearance and formatting of a blockquote.
~~Del~~	Draw a line through the selected text (strikethrough).
Ins	Define text you insert in your document.
Img	Enter the URL of an image.
ul	Start an unordered list (bullet list).
ol	Start an ordered list (numbered list).
li	Define an item in a list.
code	Insert code.
more	Insert the More tag to split long blog posts and display only certain text on your home page and archive pages. Available only for posts, not pages.
lookup	Look up a word on Answers.com.
close tags	Close any open tags. For example, if your post includes the <ul> tag, clicking this button would insert the <\ul> tag to close it.
proofread	Check spelling, grammar, and style.
full screen	Open the Distraction Free Writing mode, a minimalist view that displays only your content and a basic toolbar.

Working with Media Files

One of the best ways to enliven your WordPress site is with media files, including images, audio, video, and other documents.

WordPress offers a lot of flexibility with media files. You can upload files from your computer, insert them from a URL, create eye-catching image galleries, and embed media from sites such as YouTube, Vimeo, SlideShare, and Twitter.

WordPress 3.5 introduced a new Media Manager, which offers a streamlined interface and other enhancements. In this latest version of WordPress, you use the Add Media button to add any type of media file to a post or page. WordPress enables you to insert a variety of file types from numerous sources (see "Understanding Media File Types" later in this chapter).

See Also

See "Specifying Media Settings" in Chapter 4, "Specifying WordPress Settings," to review the WordPress media settings you selected when you first set up WordPress.

What You'll Do

Insert an Image from Your Computer

Insert a Media File from Your Computer

Embed a Hosted Media File

Insert a Media File from a URL

Upload Files Directly to the Media Library

Insert a Media File from the Media Library

Insert an Image Gallery

View the Media Library

Edit a Media File

Understanding Media File Types

WordPress supports numerous file types, including the following:

◆ **Images**—.jpg, .jpeg, .png, and .gif

◆ **PDF Files**—.pdf (viewable with the free Adobe Reader)

◆ **Microsoft Word documents**—.doc and .docx

◆ **PowerPoint presentations**—.ppt and .pptx

◆ **PowerPoint shows**—.pps and .ppsx

◆ **OpenOffice Text documents**—.odt

◆ **Audio files** (require a Space upgrade in WordPress.com) —.mp3, .m4a, .wav, and .ogg

◆ **Videos** (require the VideoPress upgrade in WordPress.com) —.mp4, .m4v, .mov, .wmv, .avi, .mpg, .ogv, .3gp, and .3g2

If you use WordPress.com, the maximum upload file size is 1GB with a total of 3GB storage. If you require more storage or want to upload audio or video, you must purchase an upgrade.

If you use self-hosted WordPress, the maximum upload file size is 64MB, but you can upload larger files via FTP. In addition, your web host might also have storage or file size limits.

See Also

See Chapter 15, "Using WordPress. com Premium Features," for more information about purchasing upgrades.

Inserting an Image from Your Computer

Inserting an image into a WordPress post or page is a fast and easy process.

Insert an Image from Your Computer

1. From the main navigation menu, select **Posts**, **Add New**. (If you want to add an image to a page, select **Pages**, **Add New**).

2. Click the **Add Media** button.

3. Click the **Upload Files** tab if it isn't already selected.

4. Click the **Select Files** button.

> **TIMESAVER** *Another option is to drag media files from your computer and drop them on the Insert Media screen. For example, you can drag files from the File Explorer if you use Windows 8.*

Did You Know?

You can also insert an image into an existing post or page. To open an existing post, click the **Edit** link below a post on the Posts screen (select **Posts**, **All Posts** from the main navigation menu). To open an existing page, click the **Edit** link below a page on the Pages screen (select **Pages**, **All Pages**).

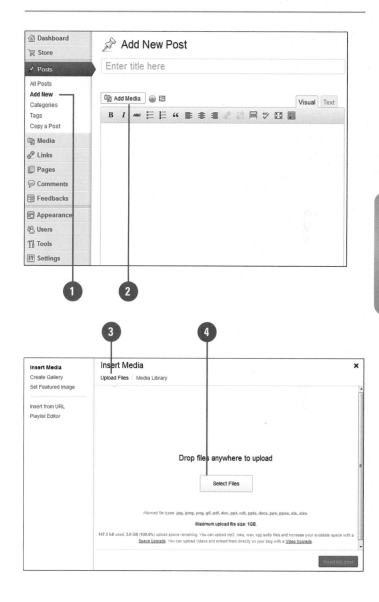

5 Select the file you want to insert and click the **Open** button.

5

Did You Know?

You can select multiple media files in the box by holding down the Shift key as you click to select files. If the images aren't contiguous, hold down the Ctrl key.

6 On the Insert Media screen, enter a Title, Caption, Alt Text, and Description for your file.

IMPORTANT *Be sure to give every image a relevant filename, title, and alt text (short for alternative text and used primarily for visually impaired site visitors). For example, if your image's filename is 123456.jpg, that doesn't give search engines any clue about your image. Using a filename such as seafood-paella-recipes.jpg and a title of "Seafood Paella Recipe" is much more meaningful. Captions (which display below your image) and descriptions are optional.*

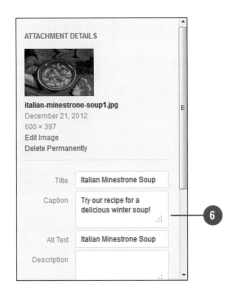

6

7 Specify file alignment: Left, Center, Right, or None.

8 Select your preferred linking option from the Link To drop-down list.

9 Specify a file size: Full Size, Large Size, Medium Size, or Thumbnail (small square). WordPress indicates the exact dimensions of each.

10 Click the **Insert into Post** button. (If you're creating a page, this button is called **Insert into Page.**)

Did You Know?

By optimizing images before uploading them, you can reduce their file sizes (pixel width and height) and decrease the time it takes to load your content. For example, rather than post a large image from your digital camera directly on WordPress, you can save it for the Web in a photo-editing application such as Photoshop or Photoshop Elements. If you use self-hosted WordPress, consider a plugin such as CW Image Optimizer (http://wordpress.org/extend/plugins/cw-image-optimizer/) if you upload a lot of images.

Did You Know?

You can easily edit or delete your image. Select the image on the Visual tab when adding/editing a post or page and click the **Edit Image** button to edit it, or click the **Delete Image** button to delete.

600 × 397
Edit Image —————————— Edit image
Delete Permanently ————————— Delete image

Title — Italian Minestrone Soup
Caption — Try our recipe for a delicious winter soup!
Alt Text — Italian Minestrone Soup
Description

ATTACHMENT DISPLAY SETTINGS
Alignment — Left — **7**
Link To — None — **8**
Size — Medium – 300 × 198 — **9**

Insert into post

10

For Your Information

WordPress Media Linking Options

WordPress offers several linking options for media files. These include

◆ **Custom URL** (link to an external website)

◆ **Attachment Page** (link to the media attachment page with file details)

◆ **Media File** (link to the full-size media file)

◆ **None** (don't link at all)

Inserting a Media File from Your Computer

In addition to inserting images, you can also insert other files, such as Word documents, PowerPoint presentations, Excel workbooks, OpenOffice documents, and PDFs.

Insert a Media File from Your Computer

1. From the main navigation menu, select **Pages**, **Add New**. (If you want to add a media file to a post, select **Posts**, **Add New**).

2. Click the **Add Media** button.

3. Click the **Upload Files** tab if it isn't already selected.

4. Click the **Select Files** button.

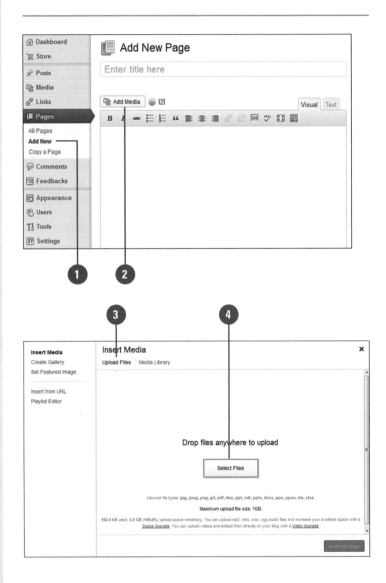

5 Select the file you want to insert and click the **Open** button.

6 On the Insert Media screen, enter a Title and optional Caption and Description for your file.

7 If you want to link your file to a URL, select one of the following from the Link To drop-down list: Custom URL, Attachment Page, or Media File.

8 Click the **Insert into Page** button (if you're creating a post, this button is called **Insert into Post**).

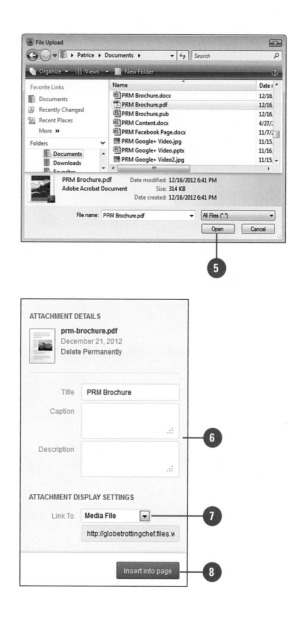

Inserting Audio Files

The options available for inserting audio files differ depending on whether you're using the hosted or self-hosted version of WordPress.

If you're using WordPress.com, you must purchase a Space upgrade to increase your storage space and upload audio files. The annual fee for this upgrade varies based on the amount of storage space you require, starting at $20 for 10GB of space.

> **TIMESAVER** *If you want to insert audio that's already hosted on the Web, you can use the audio short code [audio URL]. Here's an example: [audio http://www.patricerutledge.com/WordPress_SEO_Tips.mp3]. Note that this short code works only with WordPress.com.*

If you installed WordPress from WordPress.org, you don't need to pay to upload audio files.

With self-hosted WordPress, the easiest way to use audio is by installing a plugin that displays an audio player on your post or page, such as Audio Player (http://wordpress.org/extend/plugins/audio-player.) After uploading your audio file to the Media Library, use the following syntax to insert your file and a player in your post or page:

```
[audio:http://www.yourdomain.com/path/to/
your_mp3_file.mp3]
```

For example:

```
[audio:http://www.patricerutledge.com/
wp-content/uploads/2012/12/
WordPress_SEO_Tips.mp3]
```

If you host your audio on an external website, this site should provide code that you can embed in a WordPress post, page, or sidebar to play your audio file.

If you're a podcaster, check out the Blubrry PowerPress Podcasting plugin (http://wordpress.org/extend/plugins/powerpress), which offers iTunes support, media players, and more for podcasters who use WordPress.

> **See Also**
> See Chapter 15 for more information about purchasing upgrades.

> **See Also**
> See Chapter 12, "Working with Plugins (WordPress.org)," for more information about installing and using plugins.

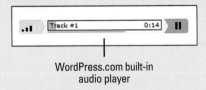

WordPress.com built-in
audio player

Inserting Videos

The options available for inserting videos differ depending on whether you're using the hosted or self-hosted version of WordPress.

If you're using WordPress.com, you must purchase the VideoPress upgrade to upload videos. The annual fee for this upgrade is $60. If you require more than 3GB of space for your videos, you can also purchase a Space upgrade.

If you installed WordPress from WordPress.org, you don't need to pay to upload videos.

IMPORTANT *Because of the large file size of most videos, you should consider other options before uploading videos directly to WordPress. For example, you can easily embed videos from sites such as YouTube and Vimeo. See "Embedding a Hosted Media File" later in this chapter for more information.*

See Also

See Chapter 15 for more information about purchasing upgrades.

Embedded YouTube video —

Embedding a Hosted Media File

WordPress makes it easy to embed media that's hosted on a variety of popular sites such as YouTube or Twitter.

Embed a Twitter Tweet

1. From the main navigation menu, select **Posts**, **Add New**. (If you want to add a media file to a page, select **Pages**, **Add New**).

2. Enter your URL in the location where you want to display the embedded media file.

   IMPORTANT *Be sure that your URL is on a single line and isn't hyperlinked (click the **Unlink** button to remove a link).*

3. Click the **Preview** button to preview your embedded file.

4. WordPress displays your embedded media file in another window.

   TIMESAVER *The easiest way to accurately insert a URL, particularly a long one, is to copy and paste it.*

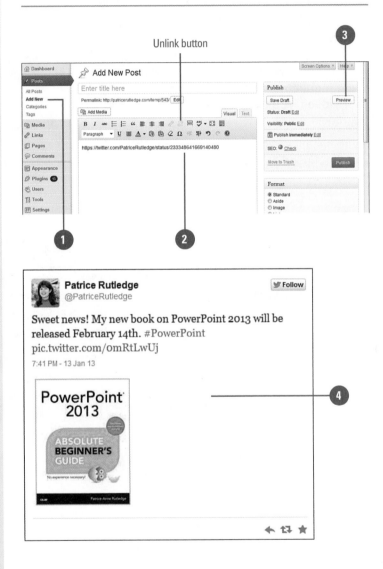

Inserting a Media File from a URL

WordPress also enables you to insert files directly from a URL. This technique is most useful if the file you want to insert is already uploaded to another website that isn't on WordPress's list of sites that support automatic embedding (see "Embedding a Hosted Media File" earlier in this chapter).

Insert a Media File from a URL

1. From the main navigation menu, select **Posts**, **Add New**. (If you want to add a media file to a page, select **Pages**, **Add New**).

2. Click the **Add Media** button.

3. Click the **Insert from URL** link.

4. Enter the file URL, starting with http://.

5. Enter a title for your file.

6. Click the **Insert into Post** button (if you're creating a page, this button is called **Insert into Page**).

Uploading Files Directly to the Media Library

If you have a large number of files you want to upload to the Media Library, you can do this all at once. Then you can insert images and other media into posts and pages directly from the Media Library whenever you need them.

Upload Files Directly to the Media Library

1. From the main navigation menu, select **Media**, **Add New**.

2. Click the **Select Files** button.

   IMPORTANT *If you use self-hosted WordPress, the Upload New Media screen has a slightly different appearance than this example from WordPress.com, but the process for uploading files is the same.*

3. Select the files you want to upload and click the **Open** button.

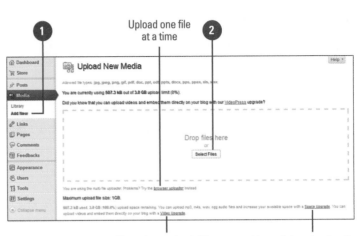

Upload one file at a time

Upgrade to upload video (WordPress.com only)

Upgrade to upload audio (WordPress.com only)

4 Click the **Edit** link to the right of each file to edit its image title, caption, alternative text, and description.

Upload New Media

Allowed file types: jpg, jpeg, png, gif, pdf, doc, ppt, odt, pptx, docx, pps, ppsx, xls, xlsx.

You are currently using **507.3 kB** out of **3.0 GB** upload limit (0%).

Did you know that you can upload videos and embed them directly on your blog with our VideoPress upgrade?

Drop files here
or
Select Files

You are using the multi-file uploader. Problems? Try the browser uploader instead.

Maximum upload file size: 1GB.

507.3 kB used, 3.0 GB (100.0%) upload space remaining. You can upload mp3, m4a, wav, ogg audio files and increase your available space with a **Space Upgrade**. You can upload videos and embed them directly on your blog with a **Video Upgrade**

Italian-minestrone-soup   Edit

Rasperries   Edit

Vegetable-basket   Edit

Inserting a Media File from the Media Library

You can insert media files directly from the Media Library if you've already uploaded them (either by a direct upload to the Media Library or by a previous insertion in a post or page).

Insert a Media File from the Media Library

1. From the main navigation menu, select **Posts**, **Add New**. (If you want to add a media file to a page, select **Pages**, **Add New**).

2. Click the **Add Media** button.

3. Click the **Media Library** tab if it isn't already selected.

4. Click the file (or files) you want to insert. WordPress displays a check mark in the upper-right corner to let you know the file is selected.

   TIMESAVER *If your Media Library contains numerous files, you can search for the right one by entering a keyword in the Search box. You can also filter media files in the drop-down list. For example, you can display only images, audio files, videos, or files previously uploaded to your current post or page.*

5. Make any changes to the attachment details or display settings, such as title, caption, alignment, linking, or size. See "Inserting an Image from Your Computer" earlier in this chapter for a reminder about these settings.

6. Click the **Insert into Post** button (if you're creating a page, this button is called **Insert into Page**).

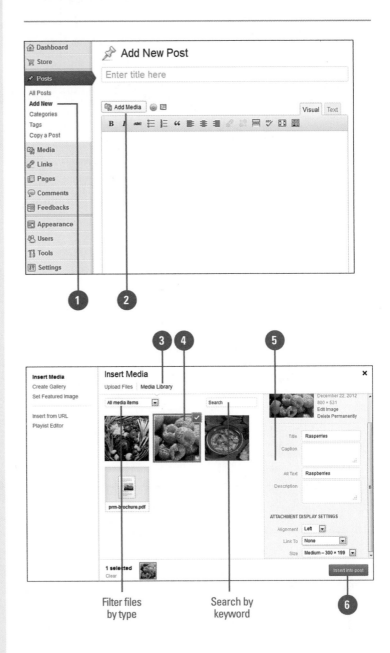

Filter files by type

Search by keyword

Inserting an Image Gallery

Inserting an image gallery is a great way to showcase a series of related images. For example, you could create a gallery for an event, for a trip, or even to represent a specific theme.

Insert an Image Gallery

1. From the main navigation menu, select **Posts**, **Add New**. (If you want to add a media file to a page, select **Pages**, **Add New**).

2. Click the **Add Media** button.

3. Click **Create Gallery**.

4. Click the **Upload Files** tab if it isn't already selected.

   TIMESAVER *You can also create a gallery from files already uploaded to the Media Library by clicking the **Media Library** tab.*

5. Click the **Select Files** button.

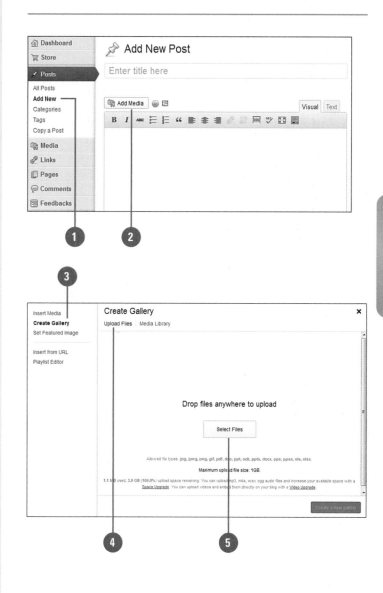

6 Select the files you want to insert and click the **Open** button.

7 On the Create Gallery screen, enter the Title and Alt Text for each image you uploaded, as well as an optional Caption and Description.

8 Click the **Create a New Gallery** button.

Did You Know?

WordPress identifies the images to include in the gallery with a check mark in the upper-right corner. If your Media Library contains other images you previously uploaded, they display on the Create Gallery screen as well, but they don't include a check mark. If you want to add one of these images to your gallery, click it to add to the gallery.

9 Optionally, drag and drop the images to reorder them.

10 Specify whether you want to link to the attachment page or the media file.

11 Select the number of columns to display (three is the default).

12 Select the **Random Order** check box if you want to display the images in random order.

13 Select a gallery type. You can accept the default (a thumbnail grid) or select one of the following: (rectangular) Tiles, Square Tiles, Circles, or Slideshow.

IMPORTANT *Gallery types are available only on WordPress.com. Self-hosted WordPress displays the default gallery style, unless you use a plugin with more sophisticated gallery options. If you use self-hosted WordPress, you can install the Jetpack plugin (http://wordpress.org/extend/plugins/jetpack/) to access this feature.*

14 Click the **Insert Gallery** button to return to the post or page.

15 Click the **Preview** button.

16 WordPress displays the gallery in another window.

Did You Know?

You can easily edit or delete your gallery. To do so, select the gallery on the Visual tab and click the **Edit Gallery** button to edit or the **Delete Gallery** button to delete.

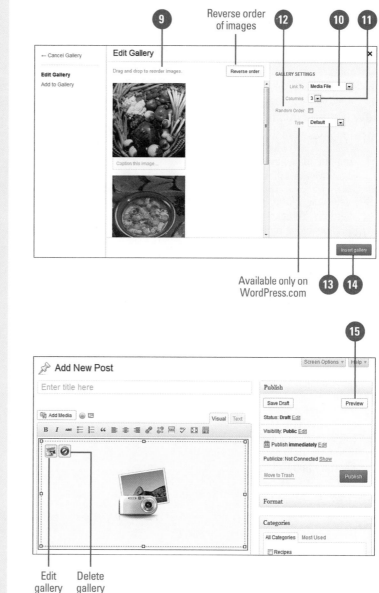

Reverse order of images

Available only on WordPress.com

Edit gallery   Delete gallery

Viewing the Media Library

On the Media Library screen, you can view all your media files in one place. If you have only a few files, it's easy to find the one you want. On the other hand, if your site contains numerous media files, Word-Press offers several options for filtering, searching, and sorting to find exactly what you're looking for.

View Media Files in the Media Library

1. From the main navigation menu, select **Media, Library**.

2. By default, WordPress displays all your files. You can filter by file type by clicking one of the following links at the top of the screen: **Image**, **Audio**, **Video**, or **Unattached** (files not attached to a post or page).

3. Click the **File**, **Author**, or **Date** heading to sort your files by this criteria.

4. If you want to filter your media files by date, select the month and year from the **Show All Dates** drop-down list and click the **Filter** button.

5. If you have a large number of files, enter keywords related to the file you want to find in the text box in the upper-right corner and click the **Search Media** button.

6. Pause your mouse over the file and click the **Edit** link to edit the file.

7. Pause your mouse over the file and click the **Delete Permanently** link to delete the file.

   TIMESAVER *To delete multiple files, select the check box to the left of each file you're deleting, select **Delete Permanently** from the Bulk Actions drop-down list, and click the **Apply** button.*

8. Pause your mouse over the file and click the **View** link to view the file.

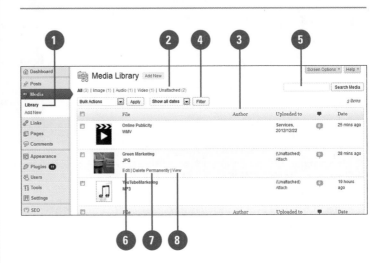

Editing a Media File

If you decide that a media file's title, caption, alt text, or description isn't quite right, you can edit it. WordPress also offers a collection of image-editing features that enable you to crop, rotate, resize, scale, and flip images. For more substantial image editing, you need to use an application such as Photoshop or Photoshop Elements.

Edit a Media File

1. From the main navigation menu, select **Media**, **Library**.

2. Pause your mouse over the file you want to edit and click the **Edit** link to open the Edit Media screen.

3. Edit any file details, including the title, caption, alternative text (only for images), and description.

4. Optionally, click the **Edit Image** button to access image-editing features. This button is available only for images.

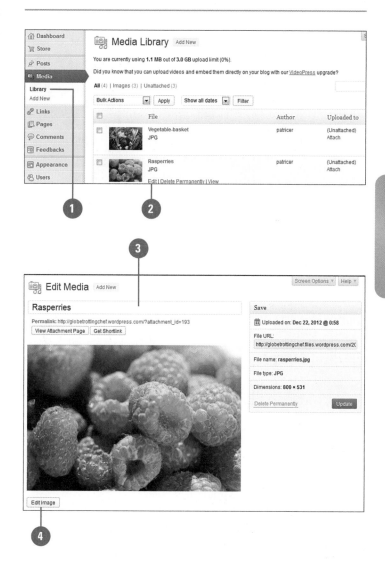

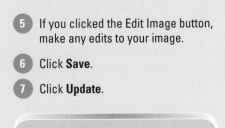

⑤ If you clicked the Edit Image button, make any edits to your image.

⑥ Click **Save**.

⑦ Click **Update**.

Did You Know?

You can also edit a media file when working on a post or page to which it's attached. To do so, select the file on the Visual tab and click the **Edit** button to edit or the **Delete** button to delete.

Pause mouse over button to view description

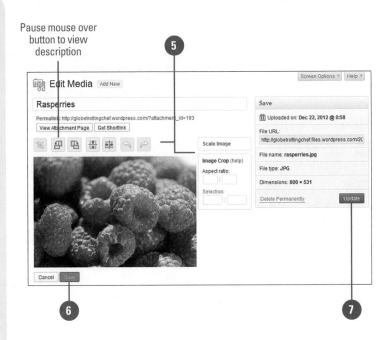

Working with Widgets

WordPress widgets enable you to add content to your website sidebars. For example, you can use widgets to display information about yourself or your business, contact details, blog categories, your latest posts, links or buttons to your site feed or external sites, your latest Twitter tweets, a Facebook Like box, images, advertising, and much more.

The biggest advantage to using WordPress widgets is their flexibility. With a little imagination, you can display almost anything you want in your sidebars.

Did You Know?

Your installed WordPress theme controls the number and placement of sidebars. The WordPress default theme Twenty Twelve, for example, includes a Main Sidebar (displayed on the right side of the page), First Front Page Widget Area, and Second Front Page Widget Area. Other themes could include a left sidebar, multiple sidebars (such as two right sidebars), or widget areas in other parts of your website, such as one or more footers at the bottom of the page. WordPress enables you to place content in any of these supported areas using widgets. Although some WordPress themes don't support widgets, most newer themes are widget ready.

What You'll Do

Add a Widget to a Sidebar

Configure a Widget

Rearrange Widgets

Remove a Widget from a Sidebar

Adding a Widget to a Sidebar

WordPress makes adding widgets drag-and-drop simple. The difficult part is deciding which widgets to use and where to place them.

Add a Widget to a Sidebar

1. From the main navigation menu, select **Appearance**, **Widgets**.

2. If the sidebar where you want to place the widget is closed, click the down arrow to its right to open it.

3. Drag a widget from either the Available Widgets section or the Inactive Widgets section on the Widgets screen.

4. Drop the widget in the sidebar location where you want to place it.

IMPORTANT *As you drag your widget to a sidebar, WordPress displays a box with a dashed line to let you know where you're placing it. Knowing the position of a widget is particularly important if the sidebar already contains other widgets and you want to display them in a specific order.*

Did You Know?

The Inactive Widgets section displays widgets you've used and removed. WordPress retains the widgets' configuration settings in case you want to use them again. This section is empty until you drag a configured widget from a sidebar to save it here. The Active Widgets section displays all available widgets.

See Also

See "Configuring a Widget" later in this chapter to learn how to config- ure the widget you just added.

Choosing the Right Widgets for Your Website

With all the widgets available for WordPress, choosing the right ones for your website is often overwhelming. Here are three helpful tips to make this task a little easier.

◆ **Choose widgets that align with your site goals**—When you first mapped out your website, you learned to align site content with site goals. This also holds true when choosing widgets to display on your sidebars. Just because something looks fun or interesting doesn't make it a good choice. Think carefully about what you want to convey to your site visitors and what actions you want them to take when considering a possible widget.

◆ **Visit other sites to get inspiration**—Even if you're creating your first website, you've most likely visited numerous existing sites and are familiar with the types of sidebar content they display. Go back to some of your favorite sites—or those of your competitors—with a more critical eye to analyze their sidebar content. What content do they display? What content is most effective? What doesn't really add much value? It's not a good idea to copy anyone directly, but a little research can provide a lot of inspiration for your own site.

◆ **Don't go overboard**—It's not hard to go overboard with widgets. Everyone has seen sites jammed with multiple sidebars filled with every widget imaginable. With widgets, however, less is often more. By aiming for the most strategic sidebar content, you can focus your readers on what you most want them to see rather than confusing them with too many options.

TIMESAVER *Plan ahead which widgets you want to use on your site and where you want to place them. Then when you're ready to create your site, you can design your sidebars quickly.*

Exploring Widgets (WordPress.com)

WordPress.com comes with the following default sidebar widgets: Search, Recent Posts, Archives, Categories, Meta, and Links. In addition, the Available Widgets section on the Widgets screen includes a solid collection of more than 40 other widgets you can use.

Some widgets worth considering include the following:

- **Categories**—Displays a list of blog categories, either individually or as a drop-down list.

- **Contact Info**—Displays your business address, phone number, and a Google map. This widget is ideal for a local business with a physical presence. If you're a home business owner, however, this one isn't for you.

- **Facebook Like Box**—Displays a Like box for your Facebook page (not a personal profile).

- **Image**—Displays an image in your sidebar. This widget requires you to enter an image URL, so your image must already be online. You can easily upload images to the WordPress Media Library and use this URL.

- **Recent Posts**—Displays your most recent posts, including an optional post date.

- **RSS Links**—Displays links or buttons to your site's Really Simple Syndication (RSS) feeds (posts, comments, or both).

- **Text**—Displays any content of your choosing that you enter as text or HTML.

- **Top Posts & Pages**—Displays your most-viewed posts and pages.

- **Twitter**—Displays up to 20 recent Twitter tweets (the default is 5). Also enables you to customize which tweets to display, including retweets and replies.

See Also

See Chapter 9, "Working with Media Files," for more information about uploading images to the WordPress Media Library.

Exploring Widgets (WordPress.org)

If you installed self-hosted WordPress and use the Twenty Twelve theme, you'll find the following default sidebar widgets with your new WordPress installation: Search, Recent Posts, Recent Comments, Archives, Categories, and Meta.

In addition, the Available Widgets section on the Widgets screen includes several other widgets you can use.

Some widgets worth considering include the following:

◆ **Categories**—Displays a list of blog categories, either individually or as a drop-down list.

◆ **RSS**—Displays a specified number of links from any RSS feed URL you enter.

◆ **Recent Posts**—Displays your most recent posts, including an optional post date.

◆ **Text**—Displays any content of your choosing that you enter as text or HTML.

After reviewing this small widget collection, you might be disappointed to learn that Word-Press.com includes far more ready-to-use widgets. Fortunately, you can duplicate the functionality of these widgets—and gain access to even more—using WordPress plugins.

TIMESAVER *The Jetpack plugin (http://wordpress.org/extend/plugins/jetpack) enables you to duplicate multiple WordPress.com features on your self-hosted WordPress site using a single plugin.*

You can search for and install plugins on the Plugins screen (click **Plugins** on the main navigation menu in self-hosted WordPress).

For example, the Social Media Widget plugin (http://wordpress.org/extend/plugins/social-media-widget/) enables you to display numerous social media icons on your sidebar. Some WordPress themes, particularly premium themes, also include widgets.

Another option is installing a plugin that enables you to customize your sidebars, such as having one sidebar for your home page and another for the remaining pages on your site. One plugin that handles this is Custom Sidebars (http://wordpress.org/extend/plugins/custom-sidebars/). Some premium themes also offer a custom sidebar plugin, such as Woo Themes (www.woothemes.com/woosidebars).

> ### See Also
>
> See Chapter 12, "Working with Plugins (WordPress.org)," and Appendix B, "WordPress Plugins," for more information about finding, installing, and managing Word-Press.org plugins.

Configuring a Widget

The steps required to configure a widget vary based on the content of each widget. This example describes how to configure the Recent Posts widget, one of the most commonly used widgets on WordPress sites.

Configure a Widget

1 From the main navigation menu, select **Appearance**, **Widgets**.

IMPORTANT *If you haven't added the Recent Posts widget to a sidebar yet, you can do so using the steps described in "Adding a Widget to a Sidebar" earlier in this chapter.*

2 If the sidebar that contains the Recent Posts widget is closed, click the down arrow to its right to open it.

3 Click the down arrow to the right of Recent Posts widget to open it.

4 Enter a title and the number of posts you want to display.

5 Optionally, select the **Display Post Date** check box if you want to display dates next to your post links.

6 Click the **Save** button to save your changes.

7 Click the **Close** link to close the widget.

Did You Know?

Some widgets have a default title you can edit. Other widgets have no title.

Did You Know?

The Text widget is the most popular WordPress widget because of its flexibility. Using this widget, you can enter text or HTML to display any content you choose on a sidebar.

Even if you don't know HTML, and don't have the time or inclination to learn it, you can still take advantage of the Text widget. For example, many popular websites—such as Facebook, LinkedIn, Twitter, YouTube, and more—provide ready-made HTML code that you can place in a sidebar.

Rearranging Widgets

After you've added several widgets, you might decide you need to rearrange them. You can rearrange widgets on a single sidebar or move a widget to another sidebar.

Rearrange Widgets

1. From the main navigation menu, select **Appearance**, **Widgets**.

2. If the sidebar whose widgets you want to rearrange is closed, click the down arrow to its right to open it.

3. Drag a widget from its existing sidebar location.

4. Drop the widget in the new sidebar location.

Removing a Widget from a Sidebar

If you decide you don't need a widget you added, you can remove it. You can also remove any of the default widgets you don't plan to use.

Remove a Widget from a Sidebar

1. From the main navigation menu, select **Appearance**, **Widgets**.

2. If the sidebar that contains the widget you want to remove is closed, click the down arrow to its right to open it.

3. Click the down arrow to the right of the widget you want to remove.

4. Click the **Delete** link.

TIMESAVER *You can also drag a widget off a sidebar to remove it.*

Did You Know?

If you want to remove a widget but retain its configuration settings for future use, you can drag it to the Inactive Widgets section at the bottom of the Widgets screen. You can reactivate this widget with its settings intact by dragging it back to a sidebar.

Working with Links

WordPress gives you the option to display links on your sidebar, including both internal and external links. For example, you could create a blogroll of your favorite websites or link to your published articles on other sites, your current clients or projects, or even specific pages or posts on your own site.

By default, WordPress includes several default links that are part of the Blogroll category, such as links to WordPress support, a theme showcase, and news. You can use these links or, optionally, delete them.

> **IMPORTANT** *The Link Manager is scheduled to be removed from WordPress in the future. At this time, you can restore the Link Manager functionality in self-hosted WordPress by using the Link Manager plugin (http://wordpress.org/extend/plugins/ link-manager/).*

What You'll Do

Create a Link Category

Add a New Link

View and Find Links

Edit Links and Link Categories

Display Links on Your Sidebar

Delete Links and Link Categories

Creating a Link Category

Before adding links to WordPress, consider how you want to categorize them and then create the appropriate link categories. For example, you could create categories for Favorite Websites, Clients, Latest Projects, or Published Articles.

Create a Link Category

1. From the main navigation menu, select **Links**, **Link Categories**.

2. On the Link Categories screen, enter a category name in the **Name** field.

3. (WordPress.org) Enter a category **Slug**. The slug displays at the end of the URL for that category and should be lowercase with only letters, numbers, and hyphens (for example, favorite-websites or latest-projects).

4. Optionally, enter a category **Description**. Some themes display this description, but not all do.

5. Click the **Add New Link Category** button. WordPress displays your new category in the box on the right side of the screen.

Adding a New Link

You can add new links quickly on the Add New Link screen.

Add a New Link

1 From the main navigation menu, select **Links**, **Add New**.

2 Enter a **Name** for your link.

3 Enter the link's complete **Web Address**, starting with http://. For example, to link to the Que Publishing website, you would enter http://www.quepublishing.com.

> **TIMESAVER** *If you're entering a long URL, you can save time and ensure accuracy by copying and pasting it into the Web Address field.*

4 Enter a link **Description**. WordPress displays this description when readers pause their mouse over this link.

5 In the **Categories** section, select the check box next to the category or categories to assign to this link.

6 Select a **Target** destination for opening your link. Your options include the following:

- **_blank**—Open the link in a new window. This option is particularly useful for links to external sites because it also keeps visitors on your site.
- **_top**—Open the link at the top level of the frame. This option is valid only if you're using frames, which I don't recommend.
- **_none**—Open the link in the same window. This is the best choice for internal links. If this link is to an external site, it takes visitors away from your site.

7 The Link Relationship section enables you to define relationships when you link to another person. If you want to let the world know that you're linking to someone who is your "crush" or "co-worker," you can click the **XFN** link for more information and complete the fields in this section. Otherwise, feel free to skip this feature.

Target

○ _blank — new window or tab.

○ _top — current window or tab, with no frames.

○ _none — same window or tab.

Choose the target frame for your link.

Link Relationship (XFN)

rel:	
identity	☐ another web address of mine
friendship	○ contact ○ acquaintance ○ friend ⦿ none
physical	☐ met
professional	☐ co-worker ☐ colleague
geographical	○ co-resident ○ neighbor ⦿ none
family	○ child ○ kin ○ parent ○ sibling ○ spouse ⦿ none
romantic	☐ muse ☐ crush ☐ date ☐ sweetheart

If the link is to a person, you can specify your relationship with them using the above form. If you would like to learn more about the idea check out XFN.

8 If you want to display an image next to your link, enter the image's URL in the **Image Address** field. Small icons sized at 16 by 16 pixels work best here.

Did You Know?

If the image you want isn't already online, you can upload it to the Word-Press Media Library, as described in Chapter 9, "Working with Media Files."

9 If you want to sort your links within a category when you display them on your sidebar, select the sort order from the **Rating** drop-down list.

10 Optionally, select the **Keep This Link Private** check box if you don't want this link to display on your sidebar with others in its category. For example, you might want to add links for future use but not display them immediately.

11 Click the **Add Link** button.

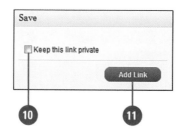

Viewing and Finding Links

On the Links screen, you can view all your WordPress links in one place. If you have only a few links, it's easy to find the link you want. If your site contains numerous links, however, WordPress offers several options for filtering, searching, and sorting to find exactly what you're looking for.

View and Find Links

① From the main navigation menu, select **Links, All Links**.

② Click the **Name, URL, Visible,** or **Ratings** heading to sort your links by this criteria.

③ If you want to filter your links by category, select the category name from the View All Categories drop-down list and click the **Filter** button.

④ If you have a large number of links, enter some text from the link in the text box in the upper-right corner and click the **Search Links** button.

⑤ Click the title of a specific link you want to view.

Editing Links and Link Categories

WordPress makes it easy to edit your links and link categories.

Edit a Link

1. From the main navigation menu, select **Links**, **All Links**.

2. On the Links screen, pause your mouse over the link you want to edit and click the **Edit** link.

3. Make any changes to the link.

4. Click the **Update Link** button to save your changes.

Edit a Link Category

1. From the main navigation menu, select **Links, Link Categories**.

2. On the Link Categories screen, pause your mouse over the category you want to edit and click the **Edit** link. The Edit Link Category screen opens.

   TIMESAVER *If you just want to change the category name or slug, click the **Quick Edit** link, make your changes, and click the **Update Link Category** button—directly on the Link Category screen.*

3. On the Edit Link Category screen, make any changes to the link category, including the name, slug, or description.

4. Click the **Update** button to save your changes.

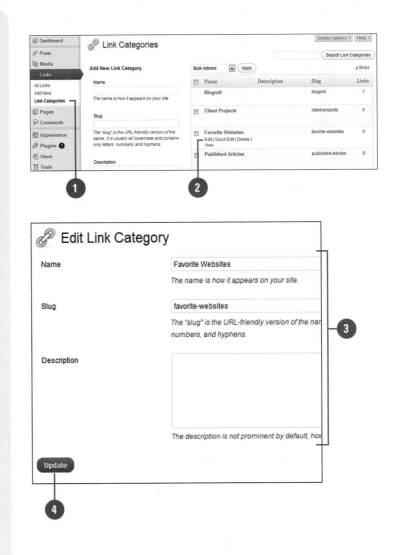

Displaying Links on Your Sidebar

When you finish adding links, you can display them on your sidebar using a widget.

Display Links on Your Sidebar

1 From the main navigation menu, select **Appearance**, **Widgets**.

2 Drag the **Links** widget to the sidebar location where you want to place it.

3 By default, WordPress displays all links. If you want to display only links for a specific category, select that category from the **Select Link Category** drop-down list.

4 To specify how you want to sort your links, select one of the following options from the **Sort By** drop-down list: Link Title (the default), Link Rating, Link ID, or Random.

5 Specify what you want to display on the sidebar by selecting any or all of the following check boxes: **Show Link Image**, **Show Link Name**, **Show Link Description**, or **Show Link Rating**. The most popular choice is to display only the link name.

6 In the **Number of Links to Show** box, enter the number of links to display on your sidebar. This is particularly useful if you have numerous links and need to limit the amount of sidebar space you use to display links.

7 Click the **Save** button. When you view your site again, the links display on your sidebar.

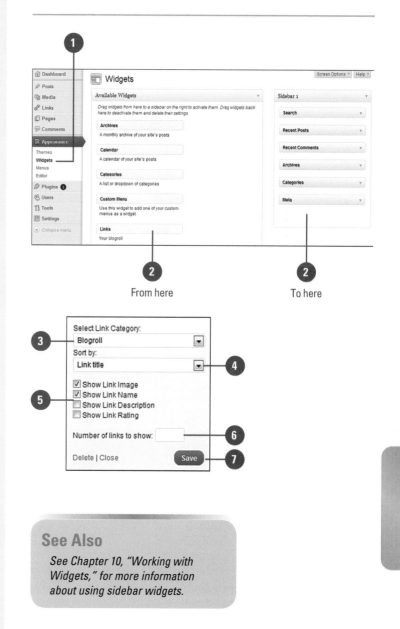

From here   To here

See Also

See Chapter 10, "Working with Widgets," for more information about using sidebar widgets.

Deleting Links and Link Categories

Deleting a WordPress link couldn't be easier; you can do so in a single click. You can also delete link categories you no longer need.

Delete a Link

① From the main navigation menu, select **Links, All Links**.

② On the Links screen, pause your mouse over the link you want to delete and click the **Delete** link below the link name. WordPress deletes the link permanently.

> **TIMESAVER** *Do you want to delete multiple links at once? Select the check box next to the links you want to delete, select* **Delete** *from the Bulk Actions drop-down list, and click the* **Apply** *button.*

Did You Know?

You can also delete a link by clicking the **Delete** link on the Edit Link screen.

Delete a Link Category

① From the main navigation menu, select **Links, All Categories**.

② On the Link Categories screen, pause your mouse over the link category you want to delete and click the **Delete** link below the link name. WordPress deletes the category permanently.

> **IMPORTANT** *You can delete only the link categories you added. You can't delete Blogroll, the default WordPress link category.*

> **TIMESAVER** *To delete multiple link categories at the same time, select the check box next to the categories you want to delete, select* **Delete** *from the Bulk Actions drop-down list, and click the* **Apply** *button.*

Working with Plugins (WordPress.org)

12

Plugins enable you to extend the power of self-hosted WordPress with additional functionality. The benefit of using plugins is that you can select only the functionality you need without overloading your WordPress site with unnecessary features.

For example, you can install and activate plugins to perform automated site backups, control spam, sell products and services, embed audio and video, display content sliders, create a membership site, enhance your site's search engine optimization (SEO), connect with social sites such as Facebook or Twitter, and much more. With more than 20,000 available plugins—and more being developed every day— one of the biggest challenges is deciding which plugins you need.

WordPress installs two plugins by default: Akismet (to control spam) and Hello Dolly (to display lyrics from the song Hello Dolly on your admin screen). I recommend activating Akismet (Hello Dolly is up to you).

What You'll Do

Search for and Install Plugins

Activate Plugins

Specify Plugin Settings

Update Plugins

Deactivate and Delete Plugins

See Also

See Appendix B, "WordPress Plugins (WordPress.org)" for a list of recommended plugins.

See Also

See "Activating the Akismet Plugin to Control Comment Spam" in Chapter 17, "Managing Comments," for more information about this plugin.

IMPORTANT *You can install plugins only on WordPress self-hosted websites. If you use WordPress.com, check out the many free and premium features that take the place of plugins (covered in Chapter 14, "Getting Feedback on Your Website (WordPress.com)," and Chapter 15, "Using WordPress.com Premium Features").*

Searching for and Installing Plugins

IMPORTANT *Be sure to perform a backup of your WordPress site before installing plugins. Most plugins install without any problems, but occasionally they might conflict with your current WordPress version or another plugin. Install one plugin at a time and verify that it installed correctly before you install another.*

Search for and Install a Plugin from the Install Plugins Screen

1. From the main navigation menu, select **Plugins**, **Add New**.

2. Enter keywords related to the type of plugin you're searching for in the text box. For example, you could enter "security" to find plugins that offer enhanced WordPress security.

   TIMESAVER *Optionally, click one of the following links to view plugins that match these criteria: Featured, Popular, or Newest. Or click one of the Popular Tags to find matching plugins.*

3. Click the **Search Plugins** button. WordPress displays a list of all plugins that match your criteria.

WordPress offers three ways to find plugins:

- Search for plugins on the Install Plugins screen and install directly from WordPress.

- Visit the WordPress Plugins Directory on wordpress.org, which includes more than 20,000 plugins for you to search, download, and install on your site. Keep in mind, however, that most of these plugins you can also download directly from WordPress itself.

- Download a free or fee-based plugin from the Web. The plugin must be in the .zip format, which is the standard for packaging plugin files.

If you download a plugin from the WordPress Plugins Directory or another website, follow the instructions in the "Uploading a Plugin" section in this chapter to activate it on your site.

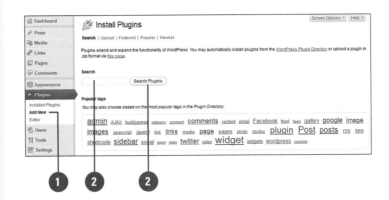

④ Click the **Details** link to view more information about a plugin, including its version number and user rating.

⑤ Click the **Install Now** link to install a plugin on your site.

⑥ In the message box that displays, click **OK**.

⑦ Click the **Activate Plugin** link to activate this plugin.

⑧ Follow any onscreen instructions for setting up the plugin. For example, WordPress often displays a link to the setup screen for a newly activated plugin. See "Specifying Plugin Settings" later in this chapter for more information.

Did You Know?

If don't want to activate this plugin now, you can activate later. See "Activating Plugins" later in this chapter for more information.

🔌 **Install Plugins**

Search | **Search Results** | Upload | Featured | Popular | I

| Tag ▾ | security | | Search Plugins |

Name	Version	Rating
BulletProof Security	.47.2	☆☆☆☆☆
Details | Install Now		
Wordfence Security	3.1.2	☆☆☆☆☆
Details | Install Now		

Are you sure you want to install this plugin?

[OK]   [Cancel]

🔌 Installing Plugin: BulletProof Security .47.2

Downloading install package from http://downloads.wordpress.org/plugin/bulletproof-security.0.47.2.zip...

Unpacking the package...

Installing the plugin...

Successfully installed the plugin **BulletProof Security .47.2**.

Activate Plugin | Return to Plugin Installer

Search for Plugins in the WordPress Plugins Directory

1 Navigate to http://wordpress.org/extend/plugins.

TIMESAVER *Click one of the links in the **Featured Plugins** section to access these plugins directly. On the sidebar, you can find links to the most popular and newest plugins.*

2 Enter keywords related to the type of plugin you're searching for in the text box. For example, you could enter "image" to find plugins that offer image functionality.

3 Click the **Search Plugins** button. WordPress displays matching plugins.

4 Click the name of a plugin to view its detail page. On this page, you can learn about the plugin's features, its rating, its number of downloads, and more.

5 Click the **Download** button to download a zipped file of this plugin to your computer. The Download button text usually includes the version number of this plugin, such as **Download Version 1.1.7**.

6 In the dialog box that opens, select the **Save File** option button and click **OK**. The options in this dialog box could vary based on your operating system and browser.

Instagrate to WordPress

Finally Instagram integration to WordPress. Automatic Instagram image posting to WordPress posts. Easy Instagration.

Instagrate to WordPress

A WordPress Plugin from *polevaultweb*

Integrate your Instagram images and your WordPress blog with automatic posting of new images into blog posts.

Download Version 1.1.7

Description | Installation | FAQ | Screenshots | Other Notes | Changelog | Stats | Support | Developers

Instagrate Pro The pro version of this plugin with many more features can be found here

The Instagrate to WordPress plugin allows you to automatically integrate your Instagram account with your WordPress blog.

No more manual embedding Instagram images into your posts, let this plugin take care of it all.

Requires: 3.0 or higher
Compatible up to: 3.4.
Last Updated: 2012-8-6
Downloads: 11,817

Average Rating

☆☆☆☆☆

5

Opening instagrate-to-wordpress.1.1.7.zip

You have chosen to open

instagrate-to-wordpress.1.1.7.zip

which is a: Compressed (zipped) Folder (888 KB)

from: http://downloads.wordpress.org

What should Firefox do with this file?

○ Open with   Windows Explorer (default)

◉ Save File

☐ Do this automatically for files like this from now on.

OK   Cancel

6

Upload a Plugin

1. From the main navigation menu, select **Plugins**, **Add New**.

2. Click the **Upload** link.

3. Click the **Browse** button.

4. Select the plugin you want to upload in the File Upload dialog box, and click the **Open** button. Depending on your operating system and browser, the names of this dialog box and button might vary.

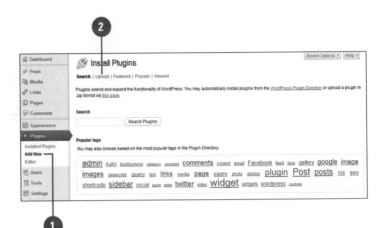

5 Click the **Install Now** button.

6 Click the **Activate Plugin** link to activate this plugin.

7 Follow any onscreen instructions for setting up the plugin. For example, WordPress often displays a link to the setup screen for a newly activated plugin. See "Specifying Plugin Settings" later in this chapter for more information.

Install Plugins

Search | **Upload** | Featured | Popular | Newest

Install a plugin in .zip format

If you have a plugin in a .zip format, you may install it by uploading it here.

C:\Users\Patrice\Dowr [Browse...] (Install Now)

5

Installing Plugin from uploaded file: woocommerce.zip

Unpacking the package...

Installing the plugin...

Plugin installed successfully.

Activate Plugin | Return to Plugins page

6

Activating Plugins

When you install a plugin, you don't have to activate it right away. You can activate—or deactivate—installed plugins at any time on the Plugins screen.

Activate a Plugin

① On the main navigation menu, click **Plugins**.

② Optionally, click the **Inactive** link to display only inactive plugins that are available for activation.

> **TIMESAVER** *You can also search for plugins by name in the text box in the upper-right corner of the screen; click the Search Installed Plugins button to filter your results. This is most useful if you have a lot of installed plugins.*

③ Click the **Activate** link below the plugin you want to activate.

④ Follow any onscreen instructions for setting up the plugin. For example, WordPress often displays a link to the setup screen for a newly activated plugin. See "Specifying Plugin Settings" later in this chapter for more information.

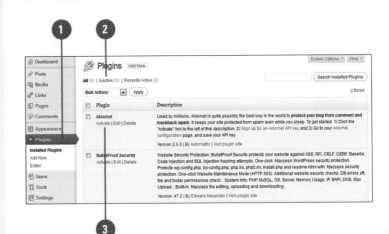

Did You Know?

Plugins that are already active won't display the Activate link; they display the Deactivate link instead.

Specifying Plugin Settings

Although some plugins start working as soon as you activate them, most require some setup. For example, many plugins add screens that you can access from the WordPress main navigation menu. You can usually find these as submenu options available from either the Settings or Tools menus. A few create menu options available on the main menu. If you know where to set up a plugin, you can go directly to that screen. Otherwise, you can access plugin settings from the Plugins screen.

Specify Plugin Settings

1. On the main navigation menu, click **Plugins**.

2. Optionally, click the **Active** link to display only active plugins.

3. Click the **Settings** link below the activated plugin you want to set up.

   TIMESAVER *Some plugins display informational text and links on the Plugins screen that let you know how to handle setup.*

4. Follow the instructions on the plugin setup screen to finish setting up your plugin.

Plugins available from the Settings menu

The Security plugin creates its own menu

For example, you can set up the Disqus plugin on the Disqus Advanced Options screen

Updating Plugins

Most plugin developers update their plugins with new functionality from time to time. For example, a plugin might require changes to take advantage of new features for WordPress or other tools it integrates with.

WordPress notifies you of the plugins you need to update in several ways:

◆ The Plugins menu option displays the number of plugins requiring updates.

◆ The WordPress Updates screen displays a list of all plugins requiring updates. Select **Dashboard**, **Updates** from the main navigation menu to view this screen.

◆ The Plugins screen displays all plugins requiring updates when you click the **Update Available** link.

Update a Plugin

1 On the main navigation menu, click **Plugins**.

2 Optionally, click the **Update Available** link to display only the plugins requiring an update.

3 Optionally, click the **View** link to view more details about this update. The View link usually includes the version number of this plugin, such as **View Version 3.4.1 Details**.

4 Click the **Update Now** link below the plugin you want to update.

Deactivating and Deleting Plugins

If you no longer want a plugin you installed, you can delete it. If you no longer want to use a plugin you activated, but don't want to delete it entirely, you can deactivate it.

Deactivate a Plugin

1. On the main navigation menu, click **Plugins**.

2. Optionally, click the **Active** link to display only active plugins that are available for deactivation.

3. Click the **Deactivate** link below the plugin you want to deactivate. WordPress deactivates the plugin but continues to display it on the Plugins screen for reactivation at a later time.

IMPORTANT *Deleting isn't the same thing as deactivating a plugin. When you delete a plugin, it's no longer available on the Plugins screen and you need to install it again to activate it.*

Delete a Plugin

1. On the main navigation menu, click **Plugins**.

2. If you haven't deactivated the plugin you want to delete, click the **Deactivate** link. The Delete link replaces the Deactivate link.

3. Click the **Delete** link below the plugin you want to delete.

4. On the Delete Plugin screen, click the **Yes, Delete These Files** button. WordPress deletes the plugin and its associated files.

Adding and
Managing Menus

Your website's menu is an important navigational tool, but a properly structured menu can do much more than direct visitors to the content on your site. The right menu can also help retain visitors and encourage sales.

TIMESAVER *If you created a sitemap for your site, as recommended in Chapter 1, "Introducing WordPress," you should already know what menus and submenus your site needs. Using this plan, you can create a menu much faster.*

By default, your WordPress menu displays a link to your home page and your site's pages in alphabetical order. If you have only a few pages, this might work just fine. If you want to customize your menu, however, there are two ways to do so:

◆ Specify page order on the Add New Page screen or Pages screen. Using the Order field, you can determine the exact order of your pages and subpages.

◆ Create a custom menu to specify page order, menu labels, and the specific items you want to display on your menu.

IMPORTANT *Although many themes support custom menus, not all do. To find a theme that offers this feature, select the **Custom Menu** check box on the Install Themes screen (WordPress. org) or the Manage Themes screen (WordPress.com). You can also search for the keywords "custom menu" in the WordPress Free Themes directory.*

See Also
See Chapter 5, "Working with Themes," for more information about searching for themes.

Changing Page Menu Order

When you create a new page, you can specify the order of this page on your menu as well as select an optional parent page. If you didn't do this, you can go back and change this setting for a specific page on the Pages screen—even after publishing.

Change Page Menu Order

1. On the main navigation menu, click **Pages**.

2. Pause your mouse over the page you want to edit and click the **Quick Edit** link to open the Quick Edit section.

3. Enter the page order in the **Order** field.

4. Optionally, select a parent page from the **Parent** drop-down list.

5. Click the **Update** button.

See Also

See "Adding a Page" in Chapter 6, "Creating and Managing Pages," for more information about specifying page menu order.

Creating Custom Menus

Creating a custom menu enables you to specify exactly which pages you do—and don't—want to display on your menu, and in which order. You can also use custom menus to add post categories and external sites to your menu and to edit menu labels.

Create a Custom Menu

1 From the main navigation menu, select **Appearance**, **Menus**.

IMPORTANT *If your current theme doesn't support custom menus, WordPress lets you know this in the Theme Locations panel (available only when you create a custom menu). You can either display your custom menu as a sidebar widget or select a new theme with menu support.*

2 Enter a name for your menu in the **Menu Name** field.

3 Click the **Create Menu** button.

4 In the Pages panel, select the check boxes next to the pages you want to add to your menu and click the **Add to Menu** button. WordPress displays only the most recent pages by default, but you can click the **View All** or **Search** tabs to find additional pages.

Did You Know?

If you've already created a custom menu and want to create another, click the **+** tab before entering a new menu name.

Did You Know?

The Home menu option is available at the top of the View All tab.

TIMESAVER *If you want to add all your pages to the menu, click the **Select All** link in the Pages panel.*

5 In the Categories panel, select the check boxes next to the post categories you want to add to your menu and click the **Add to Menu** button.

6 In the Custom Links panel, enter the URL and label of any external website you want to display on your menu and click the **Add to Menu** button. For example, if you have an external blog or portfolio, you might want to link to them on your menu.

7 Drag and drop menu items to display them in your preferred order. To create submenus, indent menu items below their parent by dragging them to the right.

Did You Know?

Adding categories to your menu is optional. One way to use this feature is to add your blog page to the menu and then add categories below this page so that your site visitors have easy access to popular categories.

Categories

Most Used | View All | Search

- ☐ Books News
- ☐ Podcasts
- ☐ Cool Apps
- ☐ PowerPoint
- ☐ Mobile Technology
- ☐ Social Media
  - ☐ LinkedIn
  - ☐ Google+
  - ☐ Facebook
- ☐ Uncategorized

Select All   (Add to Menu)

Custom Links

URL   http://

Label   Menu Item

(Add to Menu)

Home	Custom ▼
Bio	Page ▼
Books	Page ▼
Google+ in 10 Minutes	Page ▼
LinkedIn in 10 Minutes	Page ▼
PowerPoint 2010	Page ▼

8 If you want to edit a page name, click the down arrow to the right of a menu item, replace the name in the **Navigation Label** field, and click the arrow again. For example, if a page name is long, you could consider shortening it on your menu. You can also try out different navigation labels to discover which wording has the most impact on clicks and sales (if the menu item leads to a product or service).

Did You Know?

Optionally, you can enter a **Title Attribute**. This text displays when site visitors pause their mouse over a menu item.

9 If you want WordPress to add new pages to this menu automatically, select the **Automatically Add New Top-Level Pages** check box. This option can be convenient, but if your menu is highly customized, you might prefer adding menu items manually.

10 Click the **Save Menu** button.

11 Select your new menu from the **Primary Menu** drop-down list and click **Save**. This is the menu WordPress displays on your website. If you leave the Primary Menu field blank, WordPress uses your default menu.

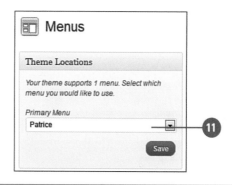

For Your Information

Advanced Customization Options

Want even more menu customization options? Click the **Screen Options** button in the upper-right corner of the screen, select the check boxes next to the optional features you want to use, and click the **Screen Options** button again to close the pull-down menu.

For example, you could select **Posts** to display selected posts on your menu. You don't want to go overboard with this, but you could highlight your most popular or important blog posts on a submenu.

Another option is to select the **Link Target** check box, which enables a new window to open when someone clicks a menu item. You should use this feature sparingly as well, but it is useful for custom links to external sites.

Managing Custom Menus

You can change a custom menu at any time, such as when you add new pages to your site. You can also edit your menu, delete menu items, or delete custom menus you no longer need.

Edit a Custom Menu

1. From the main navigation menu, select **Appearance**, **Menus**.

2. If you have more than one custom menu, select the menu you want to edit.

3. Make any changes to your menu. For example, you might want to add or delete pages, rearrange page order, and so forth.

4. Click the **Save Menu** button.

IMPORTANT *Even though most themes display only one menu at a time, you can still create multiple custom menus. For example, you could create several menus with different labels and layouts to see if this has an effect on how many people view these pages. If you might use a menu again in the future, you shouldn't delete it.*

Did You Know?

You can also add custom menus to your sidebars and footers using the Custom Menu widget. See Chapter 10, "Working with Widgets," for more information.

Delete Menu Items

1. From the main navigation menu, select **Appearance**, **Menus**.

2. If you have more than one custom menu, select the menu you want to open.

3. Click the down arrow to the right of a menu item.

4. Click the **Remove** link.

5. Click the **Save Menu** button.

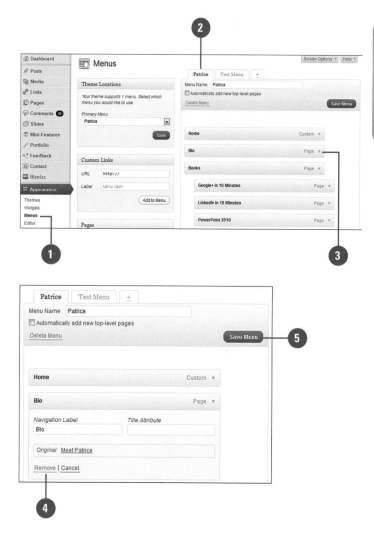

Delete a Custom Menu

① From the main navigation menu, select **Appearance**, **Menus**.

② If you have more than one custom menu, select the tab for the menu you want to delete.

③ Click the **Delete Menu** link.

④ In the message box that displays, click **OK** to confirm deletion.

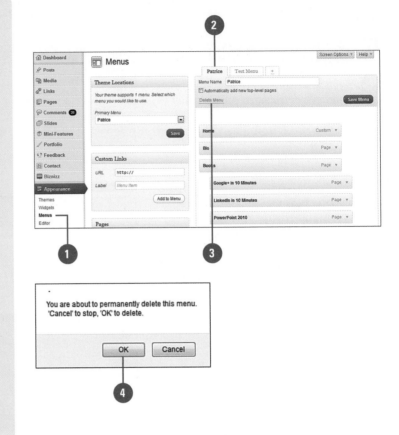

Getting Feedback on Your Website (WordPress.com)

Receiving feedback on your website—before and after publication—is an important part of its success. WordPress.com offers several built-in tools that gather feedback from both internal and external audiences.

You can receive post and page feedback from your colleagues before you publish, add polls to survey your readers about a specific topic, enable ratings on individuals posts and pages, and publish a contact form to encourage readers to contact you.

Getting Feedback on Self-Hosted WordPress Sites

If you have a self-hosted WordPress website (installed from WordPress.org), you might be disappointed to learn that the feedback tools described in this chapter are available only on WordPress.com. The good news is that you can duplicate this functionality using plugins such as the following:

◆ **Polldaddy Polls & Ratings** (http://wordpress.org/extend/plugins/polldaddy)

◆ **WP-PostRatings** (http://wordpress.org/extend/plugins/wp-postratings)

◆ **Share a Draft** (http://wordpress.org/extend/plugins/shareadraft)

◆ **Contact Form 7** (http://wordpress.org/extend/plugins/contact-form-7)

◆ **Jetpack** (http://wordpress.org/extend/plugins/jetpack)

Getting Feedback Before You Publish

WordPress.com enables you to request feedback from selected people on your posts and pages before you publish them. For example, you might need to get feedback or approval from colleagues, an editor, or your boss before publication.

You can request feedback on any unpublished post or page. When you request feedback, WordPress sends an email to the people you specified as reviewers. After a reviewer responds, WordPress sends you a notification email with a link to the post or page on which you received feedback.

Request Feedback

1. From the main navigation menu, select **Posts**, **Add New**. (If you want to request feedback on a new page, select **Pages**, **Add New**).

2. Enter your post content.

3. Click the **Request Feedback** widget.

   IMPORTANT *The Request Feedback widget displays only on unpublished posts and pages (those with a status of Draft or Pending Review). If your content hasn't been published and this widget still doesn't display on your screen, click the **Screen Options** button in the upper-right corner and verify that the **Writing Helper** check box is selected.*

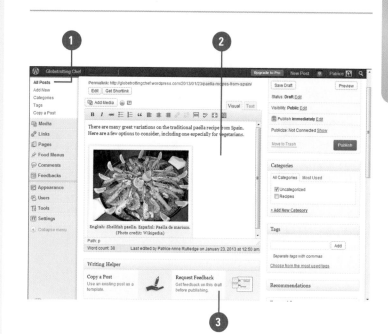

4 Enter the email addresses of the people you want to request feedback from.

5 Optionally, click the **Customize the Message** link if you want to edit the message WordPress sends to your recipients.

> **IMPORTANT** *If you want to customize your message, be careful not to delete the code [feedback-link]. This is the link your message recipients use to view and provide feedback on your content. Without this code, WordPress won't send your feedback request.*

6 Click the **Send Requests** button.

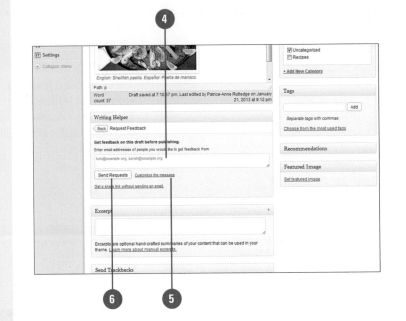

Did You Know?

If you would rather share a link directly with reviewers, click the **Get a Share Link Without Sending an Email** link. You can share this link via instant message or in your own email.

Provide Feedback

IMPORTANT *In this example, you explore the feedback process from the perspective of the reviewer.*

1 In the email you receive requesting feedback, click the link to the WordPress content you need to review.

2 Review the draft on the right side of the screen.

3 Enter your feedback in the text box.

4 Click the **Send Feedback** button.

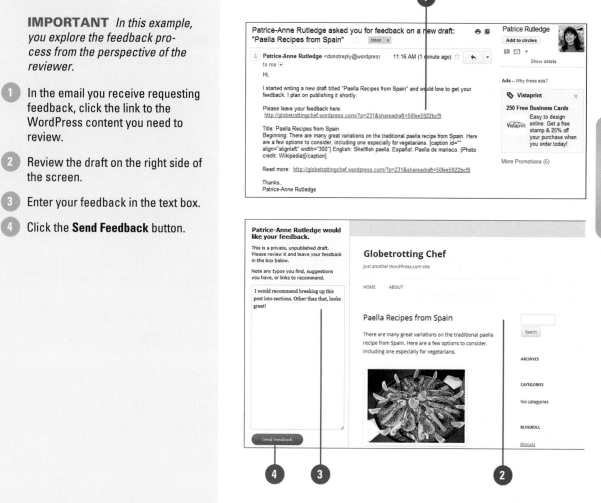

View Feedback

1. In the notification email, click the link to view feedback detail.

2. WordPress opens the related post or page where you can view the full commentary.

Hi Patrice-Anne Rutledge,

Your friend Sara Wretstrom has read your draft titled "Paella Recipes from Spain" and provided feedback for you to read:

I would recommend breaking up this post into sections. Other than that, looks great!

You can also see their feedback here:
http://globetrottingchef.wordpress.com/wp-admin/post.php?post=231&action=edit&requestfeedback=1#requestfeedback

Thanks for flying with WordPress.com

Writing Helper

‹ Back Request Feedback

Get feedback on this draft before publishing.
Enter email addresses of people you would like to get feedback from:

bob@example.org, sarah@example.org

[Send Requests] Customize the message

Get a share link without sending an email.

⬚ sara.wretstrom1@gmail.com

January 22, 2013 | Link | Revoke Access ──────

[+] I would recommend breaking up this post into sections. Other than that...

Revoke access to prevent future feedback

Working with Polls

WordPress.com integrates with Polldaddy (http://polldaddy.com), an online survey application that enables you to add interactive polls to your posts and pages.

You can add a poll directly to a post or page using the Add Poll button or embed an existing poll in a post or page.

If you want to display a poll on your website sidebar, you can add the poll shortcode to a text widget.

On the Polldaddy Polls screen, you can view all your polls in one place. On this screen, you can also edit, embed, close, preview, and delete polls.

Select a poll option

Record a vote   View poll results

Add a Poll

1 From the main navigation menu, select **Posts, Add New**. (If you want to add a poll to a page, select **Pages, Add New**).

Did You Know?

You can also add a poll to an existing post or page. To open an existing post, click the **Edit** link below a post on the Posts screen (select **Posts, All Posts** from the main navigation menu). To open an existing page, click the **Edit** link below a page on the Pages screen (select **Pages, All Pages**).

2 Click the **Add Poll** button.

What's Your Favorite Food?

Posted on January 23, 2013 by Patrice-Anne Rutledge

☆☆☆☆☆ **⊘** Rate This

What's your favorite food?

Italian	50% (1 votes)
Indian	50% (1 votes)
Japanese	0% (0 votes)
French	0% (0 votes)
Mexican	0% (0 votes)

Total Votes: 2

▪ Like ⟨ 0

▪ Tweet ⟨ 0

Comments (0)   Return To Poll

Create Your Own Poll

Poll results

Like poll on Facebook

Share poll on Twitter

Add New Post

Enter title here

📷 Add Media

B I | Visual | Text

Publish

Save Draft | Preview

Status: Draft Edit

Visibility: Public Edit

Publish immediately Edit

Publicize: Not Connected Show

Move to Trash | Publish

Format

Categories

All Categories | Most Used

☐ Recipes
☐ Uncategorized

+ Add New Category

Dashboard
Store
Posts
  All Posts
  Add New
  Categories
  Tags
  Copy a Post
Media
Links
Pages
Comments
Feedbacks
Appearance
Users
Tools
Settings
Collapse menu

Path: p
Word count: 0

Screen Options ▾ | Help ▾

③ Select the **Auto-Create a New Account (Recommended)** option button.

IMPORTANT *If you've already created a poll, WordPress displays a list of your existing polls. You can insert one of these existing polls or click the **Add New** button to add a new poll and continue to step 6.*

④ Click the **Do It: I Want Some Polls!** button.

⑤ Click the **Create a Poll Now** button.

Did You Know?

If you already have an existing Polldaddy account, you can import your account data into WordPress by selecting the **Import My Existing Polldaddy Account** option button.

Add Poll   ✕

🎯 Polls in WordPress

To use polls in WordPress, you will need an account with our sister product, Polldaddy.com.

③ ──── ⦿ Auto-create a new account (recommended).

○ Import my existing PollDaddy account.

④ ──── Do it: I want some polls!

Thank you for creating with WordPress • Support • Forums • Learn WordPress — Tutorials and Walkthroughs

---

Add Poll   ✕

🎯 Polldaddy Polls   Add New

Account Imported.

Actions ▾   Apply   View All Polls ▾   Filter

☐ Poll

You haven't used our fancy plugin to create any polls for this blog!
Why don't you go ahead and get started on that?

⑤ ──── Create a Poll Now

Thank you for creating with WordPress • Support • Forums • Learn WordPress — Tutorials and Walkthroughs

6 Enter a title for your poll.

7 Enter potential answers in the Answers box. If you need additional answers, click the **Add New Answer** button.

8 Specify your preferred save options, such as random answer display, allowing users to enter other answers, multiple choice answers, or poll sharing.

9 Select a poll style and width. By default, your poll uses a medium-sized Plain White style.

10 Specify whether you want to display poll results, percentages only, or no results.

11 Specify whether you want to block repeat voting and for how long.

Did You Know?

Blocking repeat voting can keep your poll results clean.

12 Specify whether you want to allow comments on your poll. If you do allow comments, you can moderate them first to avoid spam or unprofessional content.

13 Click the **Save Poll** button.

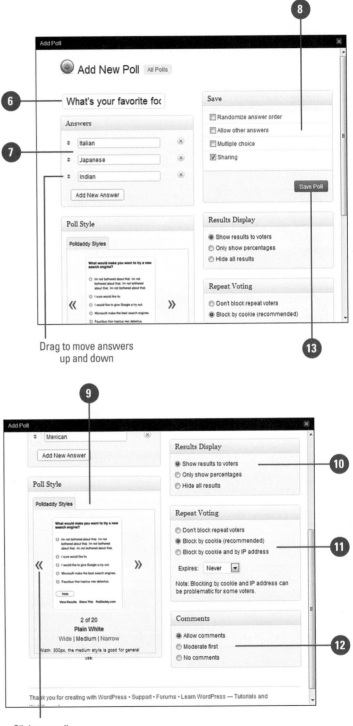

Drag to move answers up and down

Click to scroll through styles

14 Click the **Embed in Post** button.

TIMESAVER *Specify your default poll settings on the Poll Settings screen (click **Settings**, **Polls** from the main navigation menu). All future polls display these settings without your having to make any selections.*

Did You Know?

WordPress embeds your poll into your post as a shortcode, such as [polldaddy poll=6848242]. After embedding your poll, you can add more content to your post, click the **Preview** button to preview it in a browser, and then either save it as a draft or publish it to the Web.

Did You Know?

You can also create a new poll by clicking the **Add New** button on the Polldaddy Polls screen (see "View and Manage Polls" later in this chapter for more information about this screen). Using this method enables you to add audio and video to your polls.

Insert an Existing Poll

1 From the main navigation menu, select **Pages, Add New**.

2 Click the **Add Poll** button.

3 Pause the mouse over the poll you want to insert and click the **Embed in Post** link.

4 WordPress adds the poll shortcode to the page.

Add a Poll to a Sidebar

1 From the main navigation menu, select **Feedbacks**, **Polls**.

2 Pause the mouse over the poll you want to display and click the **Embed & Link** link.

3 Select the **WordPress Shortcode** and press Ctrl+C to copy it.

See Also

See Chapter 10, "Working with Widgets," for more information about using text widgets.

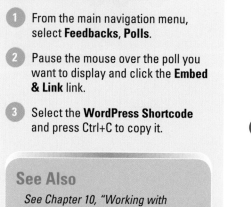

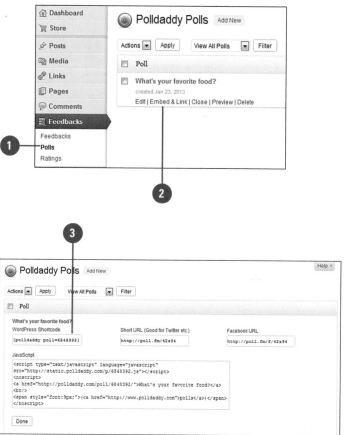

4 From the main navigation menu, select **Appearance**, **Widgets**.

5 Drag the Text widget to the sidebar location where you want to place it. The widget opens.

6 Add an optional title.

7 Press Ctrl+P to paste the poll shortcode in the text box.

8 Click the **Save** button.

9 Click the **Close** link to close the widget.

IMPORTANT *Be sure to preview the poll on your sidebar to verify that it fits. If the poll is too wide, you can edit its size (see "View and Manage Polls" later in this chapter).*

IMPORTANT *A poll can display only once on a single screen. For example, if you create a post that contains a poll and then add the same poll to your sidebar, viewers reading that post can view the poll only in the post, not in the sidebar. The instance you created first is the one that displays. On a post or page without the poll, the sidebar poll displays again. To avoid this problem, create unique polls for your sidebar.*

View and Manage Polls

1 From the main navigation menu, select **Feedbacks**, **Polls**.

2 Pause your mouse over a poll and click the **Edit** link to edit it. For example, you can fix a poll typo or change its size or style.

3 Pause your mouse over a poll and click the **Embed & Link** link to access embed codes and links for your poll.

4 Pause your mouse over a poll and click the **Close** link to close it and not accept any further votes.

5 Pause your mouse over a poll and click the **Preview** link to preview the poll as your readers would see it.

6 Pause your mouse over a poll and click the **Delete** link to delete it. WordPress prompts you to confirm the deletion.

7 Pause your mouse over a poll and click the **Results** link to view poll results.

TIMESAVER *If you want to delete, close, or open multiple polls, select the check boxes to their left, select the action you want to take from the Actions drop-down list, and then click the **Apply** button.*

Apply actions to multiple polls

Filter polls if you have multiple sites

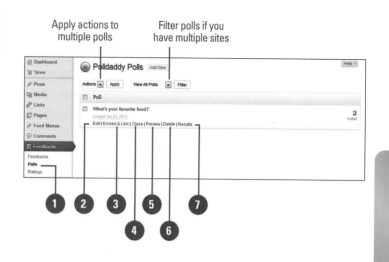

Did You Know?

You can embed a poll on a sidebar (see "Adding a Poll to a Sidebar" earlier in this chapter), post it on Twitter, or share it on Facebook using the codes Polldaddy provides.

Did You Know?

If you close a poll by mistake or change your mind, pause your mouse over it and click the **Open** link to reopen it. The Open link displays only on closed polls.

Working with Ratings

Ratings are another way to get feedback on your website content. WordPress enables your readers to rate posts, pages, and comments. (You control which, if any, of these are available to rate.) You can use the default rating options (Very Poor, Poor, Average, Good, or Excellent) or create your own.

To use the WordPress.com Ratings feature, you first need to enable it on the Rating Settings screen (select **Settings**, **Ratings** from the main navigation menu).

On the Rating Results screen, you can view, filter, and delete all your ratings in one place.

See Also

See "Setting Up Ratings" in Chapter 4, "Specifying WordPress Settings," for more information about setting up ratings.

Readers can rate your content

> ## Paella Recipes: A Spanish Tradition
>
> Leave a reply
>
> ☆☆☆☆☆ ❶ Rate This
>
> There are many great variations on the traditional paella recipe from Spain. Here are a few options to consider, including one especially for vegetarians.
>
> *English: Shellfish paella. Español: Paella de marisco.*
> *(Photo credit: Wikipedia)*

View the number of votes and average rating

> ## Paella Recipes: A Spanish Tradition
>
> Leave a reply
>
> ★★★★★ ❶ 1 Vote
>
> There are many great variations on the traditional paella recipe from Spain. Here are a few options to consider, including one especially for vegetarians.
>
> *English: Shellfish paella. Español: Paella de marisco.*
> *(Photo credit: Wikipedia)*

View and Manage Ratings

1. From the main navigation menu, select **Feedbacks, Ratings**.

2. View the number of votes and average rating for each post, page, or comment that accepts ratings.

3. If you want to filter ratings by type, select **Posts, Pages,** or **Comments** from the drop-down list and click the **Filter** button.

4. If you want to filter ratings by date, select the timeframe from the drop-down list and click the **Filter** button. Options range from the past seven days to all dates.

5. Pause your mouse over a filename and click the **Delete** link to delete its rating. WordPress prompts you to confirm the deletion.

> **TIMESAVER** *If you want to delete multiple ratings, select the check boxes to their left, select **Delete** from the Actions drop-down list, and then click the **Apply** button.*

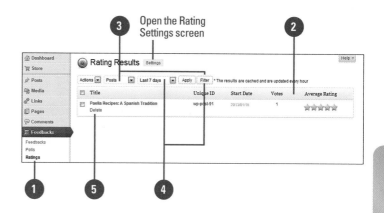

Open the Rating Settings screen

Working with Contact Forms

With WordPress.com, you can add a contact form to a post or page. Creating a "Contact Us" page is a popular way to encourage feedback from your site visitors.

You can place a contact form on a WordPress page or post in less than a minute if you accept the default fields. If you want to customize your form, you can do so by editing, adding, deleting, or moving fields. You can also customize a new or existing form with additional fields.

On the Feedbacks screen, you can view the feedback you receive through your contact form (WordPress also sends you this information by email).

Add a Contact Form to a Page

1. From the main navigation menu, select **Pages**, **Add New**.

2. Click the **Add a Custom Form** button.

    TIMESAVER *If you don't want to customize your form, skip to step 8 to insert it on your page.*

Sample Contact Us page with a contact form

You can specify which fields are required

3. Review the default fields WordPress places on your contact form.

4. Pause your mouse over a field and click the **Edit** link to edit it.

5. Pause your mouse over a field and click the **Move** link to move it to another location on the form.

6. Click the **minus sign** to the right of any field to delete it.

7. Click the **Add a New Field** link to add a new field to your form. See "Add a New Field to a Contact Form" later in this chapter for more information.

8. Optionally, click the **Email Notifications** tab if you want to enter a specific email address and subject line for feedback notifications. By default, WordPress sends notifications to the author of the page or post.

9. Click the **Add This Form to My Post** button.

10. WordPress places the form code on your page, which displays as a form when you publish.

> **IMPORTANT** *Be sure to click the **Preview** button to preview your live form before you publish. You should also submit some test feedback to ensure that your form works properly. If you discover any problems, click the **Add a Custom Form** button again to edit your form.*

Add a custom form

Form builder   Email notifications

Here's what your form will look like

Name (required)   move | edit

Email (required)

Website

Comment (required)

Add a new field

Add this form to my post

How does this work?

By adding a contact form, your readers will be able to submit feedback to you. All feedback is automatically scanned for spam, and the legitimate feedback will be emailed to you.

Can I add more fields?

Sure thing. Click here to add a new text box, textarea, radio, checkbox, or dropdown field.

Can I view my feedback within WordPress?

Yep, you can read your feedback at any time by clicking the "Feedbacks" link in the admin menu.

Edit Page   Add New

Contact Us

Permalink: http://globetrottingchef.wordpress.com/contact-us/ Edit View Page — Preview your form
Get Shortlink

Add Media   Visual   Text

B I ABC

[contact-form][contact-field label='Name' type='name' required='1'/][contact-field label='Email' type='email' required='1'/][contact-field label='Website' type='url'/]
[contact-field label='Comment' type='textarea' required='1'/][/contact-form]

Add a New Field to a Contact Form

1 In an open contact form, click the **Add a New Field** link.

2 In the **Label** field, enter a name for your field.

3 Select a **Field Type** from the drop-down list. Your options include

- ◆ **Checkbox**—A single check box
- ◆ **Drop down**—A drop-down list with multiple options you can set up
- ◆ **Email**—A single line for entering an email address
- ◆ **Name**—A single line for entering a name
- ◆ **Radio**—A series of radio buttons with multiple options you can set up
- ◆ **Text**—A single line for entering text
- ◆ **Textarea**—A multiple line box for entering text
- ◆ **Website**—A single line for entering a website URL

4 Select the **Required?** check box if this is a mandatory field.

IMPORTANT *The more fields you specify as required, the less feedback you're likely to receive. Many people dislike lengthy forms that require a lot of personal information.*

5 Click the **Save This Field** button.

6 Repeat steps 1 through 5 to add another field.

7 Click **Add This Form to My Post** when you're finished adding fields.

Additional fields might display depending on the selected field type

View Contact Form Feedback

1. From the main navigation menu, select **Feedbacks**, **Feedbacks**.

2. View a list of all feedback by date.

3. If you want to filter feedback by date, select the timeframe from the drop-down list and click the **Filter** button.

4. Click the feedback link to open the feedback in a browser window where you can reply to it.

5. Pause your mouse over a feedback item and click the **Spam** link to mark the feedback as spam.

6. Pause your mouse over a feedback item and click the **Trash** link to delete the feedback.

TIMESAVER *If you want to delete multiple feedback items, select the check boxes to their left, select **Move to Trash** from the Actions drop-down list, and then click the **Apply** button.*

Restore or empty trash   Search your feedback

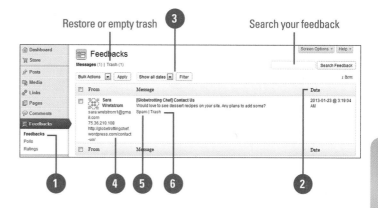

Did You Know?

After moving an item to the trash, click the **Trash** link to restore or permanently delete it.

Did You Know?

WordPress uses Akismet (http://akismet.com) to filter your feedback, which greatly reduces spam.

Did You Know?

You can also respond to feedback by responding to the email notifications you receive. This method also keeps a record of your reply in your email system.

WordPress.com Premium Features

WordPress.com offers several premium features that you can purchase. These upgrades enable you to upload audio and video to your site, register and map to a custom domain name, remove ads, increase storage space, and more.

> **IMPORTANT** *If you use self-hosted WordPress or are thinking of transferring in the future, be aware that it doesn't offer fee-based premium features (although you can purchase premium themes or plugins). Some of the WordPress.com premium features either aren't necessary (such as removing ads), are already included (the capability to upload audio and video files), or are features that come as part of your web-hosting package (mapping to a domain, storage, or site redirection).*

What You'll Do

Purchase an Upgrade

View and Manage Upgrades

View Your Billing History

Exploring WordPress.com Upgrades

WordPress.com offers numerous upgrades that extend its capabilities and functionality. In this sidebar, you explore the options available on the Store screen.

Add a Domain Upgrade

One of the most popular WordPress.com upgrades is a custom domain name for your site. This is particularly important if you use your site for business and want to project a professional, branded image. For example, by using this upgrade you could map your WordPress.com site globetrottingchef.wordpress.com to www.globetrottingchef.com.

This upgrade costs $18 per year ($13 for mapping the domain and $5 for registering the domain name). If you already registered your own domain name, the fee is only $13 for mapping.

VideoPress Upgrade

With the VideoPress upgrade, you can upload and play HD videos on your WordPress site. Priced at $60 per year, the VideoPress upgrade enables you to do the following:

◆ Upload videos up to 1GB in size with no length limit

◆ Play videos without ads

◆ Insert videos in a variety of formats including MP4 (.mp4, .m4v), QuickTime movies (.mov), Windows Media Video (.wmv), Audio Video Interleave (.avi), MPEG (.mpg), Ogg (.ogv), 3GPP (.3gp) and 3GPP2 (.3g2)

◆ Share videos from your iPhone or iPad using the WordPress App for iOS (http://ios.wordpress.org)

Custom Design Upgrade

If you aren't satisfied with your website's fonts, colors, or other design elements, you can change them using the Custom Design upgrade, priced at $30 per year. With this upgrade, you can do the following:

◆ Select from a collection of more than 50 fonts

◆ Change your site's color scheme or select the perfect color using the color picker

◆ Use the CSS Editor to customize your site's style sheet

IMPORTANT *This upgrade doesn't enable you to edit a theme directly or upload templates or custom themes. If you want to perform these advanced tasks, you should install self-hosted WordPress.*

Did You Know?

By default, your WordPress.com account provides 3GB of storage. If you require more space than this to upload videos, consider purchasing a space upgrade (described later in this sidebar).

Did You Know?

Using the CSS Editor is an advanced task that requires some knowledge of Cascading Style Sheets (CSS). WordPress style sheets use CSS to specify a theme's exact layout, fonts, color, and other design elements. You can learn more at http://en.support.wordpress.com/custom-design/css-basics.

Space Upgrade

If the default 3GB of storage space that comes with WordPress.com isn't enough to suit your needs, you can purchase a space upgrade. Pricing varies based on the space required and includes the options listed in the table.

WordPress.com Space Upgrade Pricing	
Space Upgrade	**Annual Price**
10GB	$20
25GB	$50
50GB	$90
100GB	$160
200GB	$290

Did You Know?

A space upgrade is also required if you want to upload audio files, such as podcasts, to your website. WordPress.com supports .mp3, .m4a, .wav, and .ogg files. You can also upload .zip files with this upgrade.

Did You Know?

Not sure how much space you need? 10GB is enough to upload approximately 2,000 photos or 1,000 songs. 200GB is enough space to upload about 40,000 photos or 20,000 songs. Keep in mind, however, that longer audio files and video files could require substantially more space than a photo or song.

No Ads Upgrade

To pay for the free features WordPress.com provides, text ads might display on your website. For $30 per year, however, you can remove all ads.

Site Redirect Upgrade

If you decide to leave WordPress.com for self-hosted WordPress, you can bring your existing audience with you by purchasing a Site Redirect upgrade. This upgrade, priced at $13 per year, redirects traffic from your old WordPress.com site to your new hosted site.

Did You Know?

The Site Redirect upgrade uses Search Engine Optimization (SEO)– friendly 301 permanent redirects to direct traffic to your new site. 301 is a type of HTTP status code that gives your browser instructions when someone visits a page on your site. You don't need to understand the technical details of HTTP status codes or redirects, however, to benefit from this upgrade. The most important thing to understand is the benefit this redirect provides: retaining search engine rankings from your previous site.

Premium Theme Upgrade

Although WordPress.com offers numerous free themes, you might want to upgrade to a premium theme with a specific design or more flexibility. You can choose from a variety of options, with prices starting at $50 (a one-time expense).

> **See Also**
>
> *See Chapter 5, "Working with Themes," for more information about premium themes.*

Guided Transfer Upgrade

If you decide it's time to move from your hosted WordPress.com account to a self-hosted WordPress site, you can have a WordPress "happiness engineer" handle the transfer for you for a one-time fee of $129. This service includes the following:

- ◆ Installation of WordPress using the recommended web hosting service you prefer: Bluehost, HostGator, DreamHost, or Go Daddy

- ◆ Transfer of your WordPress.com site to your new domain

- ◆ Installation and configuration of plugins that duplicate built-in WordPress.com features you're using

- ◆ Two weeks of technical support

Understanding WordPress Bundles

If you're interested in purchasing several WordPress upgrades, you can save money by purchasing a bundle.

WordPress Value Bundle

The WordPress Value Bundle offers five popular upgrades for $99 per year (a 40 percent discount). This bundle includes the following upgrades:

◆ Add a Domain

◆ No Ads

◆ VideoPress

◆ Custom Design

◆ 10GB space upgrade

WordPress.com Business

This bundle, priced at $299 per year, includes all the upgrades in the Value Bundle plus the following:

◆ Unlimited access to premium themes

◆ Unlimited uploads and storage for audio and video files

◆ Technical support via phone or live chat

◆ Custom contact forms

◆ Security monitoring and alerts

WordPress Enterprise

If you're creating a high-end, enterprise website, this bundle offers superior functionality and support for $500 per month. The Enterprise bundle includes the following:

◆ Complete site customization, including CSS, fonts, and JavaScript

◆ Unlimited storage and bandwidth

◆ Unlimited access to premium themes

◆ Website analytics such as Google Analytics or Chartbeat

◆ Access to more than 100 plugins (normally available only for self-hosted sites)

◆ The capability to place your own ads on your website without any WordPress.com ads

◆ Security monitoring and alerts

◆ Upgraded technical support

Purchasing an Upgrade

You can purchase one or more upgrades from the Store screen.

Purchase an Upgrade

1. From the main navigation menu, select **Store**, **Store**.

2. On the Store screen, click the **Buy Now** button next to the upgrade you want to purchase. This example uses the Custom Design upgrade.

   TIMESAVER *Optionally, click the **Upgrade to Pro** button in the upper-right corner of the screen to add the WordPress Value Bundle directly to your shopping cart.*

3. If this is the only upgrade you want to purchase, click the **Check Out Now** button.

4. If you want to purchase other upgrades, click the **Add to Cart & Continue Browsing** button to return to the Store screen.

Did You Know?

Click the **Learn More** button for more information about an upgrade.

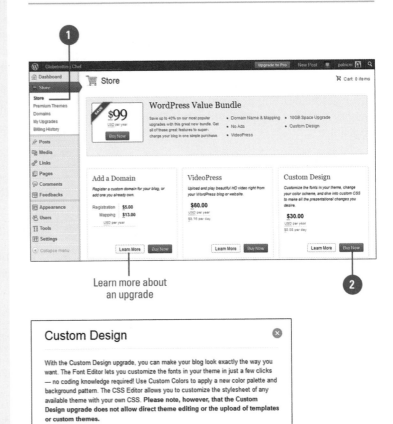

Learn more about an upgrade

5 On the My Shopping Cart screen, select a payment method and enter your payment details.

6 Click the **Purchase** button. Follow the onscreen instructions to complete your purchase, which vary by purchase method.

Did You Know?

Payment options include credit card (Visa, MasterCard, American Express, and Discover), PayPal, or Bitcoin. Bitcoin (http://bitcoin.org) is an open-source electronic currency.

Review upgrade cancellation policy

Remove an upgrade from the cart

🛒 My shopping cart

Product		Cost
Custom Design (more info) 1 year subscription	Remove from Cart	$30.00
	Total	$30.00 USD

Upgrades can be canceled for a full refund within 30 days of placing your order.

Choose a Payment Method

New Credit Card	PayPal	Bitcoin

Credit Card
○ VISA   ○ MasterCard   ○ AMEX   ○ DISCOVER

Credit Card Number   Security Code (?)

Grab the $99 bundle and save

You'll get all of this...
- ○ Domain Name
- ○ 10GB Space
- ○ No Ads
- ○ Custom Design
- ○ VideoPress

All for $99.00 (a $166.00 value)

Yes, I want the bundle!

Upgrade to the WordPress Value Bundle

☑ Remember details

Checking this will allow you to use these details for future purchases. We don't store anything confidential, so your privacy will not be affected.

WordPress.com transactions will appear on your bank or credit card statements under the name WP-FEE.COM. Please do not delete your email receipt. If possible, print it out and keep it in a safe place.

Your order will automatically renew on 2014-01-08. You can disable automatic renewals at any time.

Your upgrade subscription will automatically renew every 12 months from the date of your original purchase. We'll attempt to charge the credit card you used to make your initial upgrade purchase. You can cancel automatic renewal at any time prior to your renewal date by visiting the Upgrades section of your blog's Dashboard and clicking **Disable Auto-Renew** next to the upgrade.

We'll notify you three times by email prior to renewing a non-domain upgrade. We'll notify you 90 days and 60 days prior to renewing a domain on your behalf, and attempt to renew the domain 30 days prior to expiration.

Contact us any time with questions via support.

TOTAL
$30.00 USD

Purchase ›

Cancel

🔒 SSL Secure Connection

Review upgrade renewal policy

Viewing and Managing Upgrades

On the My Upgrades screen, you can view the upgrades you purchased, modify automatic renewal settings, and cancel upgrades.

View and Manage Your Upgrades

① From the main navigation menu, select **Store**, **My Upgrades**.

② View details about the upgrades you purchased.

③ Click the **Disable Auto Renew** link to disable automatic renewal of annual upgrades.

④ Click the **Cancel and Refund** link to cancel an upgrade and request a refund.

> **IMPORTANT** *WordPress has specific time parameters for cancellations and refunds that display on the My Shopping Cart screen before purchase. For example, you can cancel most upgrades within 30 days for a full refund. Domain renewals, however, are not refundable. New domain registrations must be cancelled within two days.*

⑤ Click the **Transfer to Another Site** link to transfer an upgrade to another WordPress.com site.

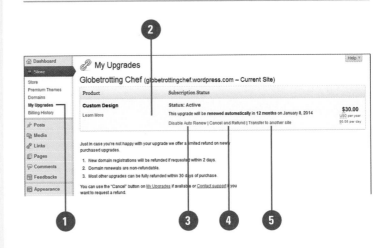

Viewing Your Billing History

You can easily view the status of purchased upgrades on the Billing History screen.

View Your Billing History

1 From the main navigation menu, select **Store**, **Billing History**.

2 View billing information for each upgrade.

3 Click the **View/Print** link to view or print a detailed receipt.

4 Click the **Email** link to send an upgrade receipt to your primary WordPress.com email address (listed on the General Settings screen).

Managing Users

Working on your WordPress website doesn't have to be a solo project. WordPress offers several user roles that give other people varying levels of access: everything from complete control of your site to the capability to create posts without actually publishing them.

Although the concept behind adding and managing users is the same whether you use WordPress.com or self-hosted WordPress, the process is slightly different. On WordPress.com, you invite new users. With self-hosted WordPress, you add them directly to your site.

Understanding User Roles

Before adding users to your WordPress system, you need to understand all available roles and the capabilities these roles provide designated users. You can assign users to any of the following roles:

◆ **Administrators**—Manage all site settings; install themes and plugins; add, manage, and delete other users; view, create, edit, publish, or delete *all* site posts and pages; manage comments, categories, tags, and links; upload media files; and delete the entire site. In other words, a site administrator has complete control over *everything*. When you create a WordPress site, this is the role you're assigned.

> **IMPORTANT** *The administrator role is a powerful one, so consider carefully before assigning this role to another person. You should limit the number of people who have admin rights and verify the WordPress experience of a potential admin, particularly someone you don't know well (such as a consultant or freelancer).*

◆ **Editors**—View, create, edit, publish, or delete *all* site posts and pages; manage comments, categories, tags, and links; upload media files.

◆ **Authors**—View, create, edit, publish, or delete their *own* posts; upload media files.

◆ **Contributors**—View, create, and edit their *own* posts before publication.

◆ **Viewers**—View a private website and add comments if you've enabled this feature. This option is available only for WordPress.com sites.

◆ **Followers**—View posts on their Read page. This option is available only for WordPress.com sites. Although people can follow your site without an invitation, by sending an invitation, you can introduce your site to people you know.

◆ **Subscribers**—Modify their profile and comment without having to enter their name or email address. This option is available only for self-hosted WordPress sites.

> **IMPORTANT** *Before adding a new user, ask yourself whether this person really needs an account on your website. For example, it usually isn't worth the effort to create an account for a one-time contributor. If you use self-hosted WordPress, consider a plugin, such as WordPress Guest Post (http://wordpress.org/extend/plugins/wordpress-guest-post), to handle guest posts.*

Did You Know?

Users have access only to the WordPress features their assigned role allows. For example, someone with Editor access won't see the Users menu because he can't manage users.

Did You Know?

Contributors can't upload media files or publish their posts. An administrator must review contributor posts and, optionally, publish them. After publication, contributors can no longer edit their posts.

Adding New Users (WordPress.com)

On WordPress.com, you must invite new users to your website. You can then manage and track the invitations you send.

Invite New Users

1. From the main navigation menu, select **Users**, **Invite New**.

2. Enter the email address or WordPress.com username of up to 10 people you want to invite, separated by commas.

3. Select the role you want to give these individuals. Options include Administrator, Editor, Author, Contributor, or Follower.

4. Enter an optional message of up to 500 characters.

5. Click the **Send Invitation** button.

6. WordPress sends the invitations and displays the invitees in the Past Invitations section at the bottom of the screen.

Did You Know?

Everyone you list in the Usernames or Email Addresses box must be assigned the same role. If you want to assign one person an Editor role and another a Contributor role, you need to complete the invitation process separately.

The WordPress.com Invitation Process

What happens after you send invitations depends on whether an invitee has an existing WordPress.com account.

Invitees who don't have an existing WordPress.com account (invitations sent to an email address), receive an email requesting them to sign up for an account (a link is provided) and then click the **Accept Invitation** button.

Invitees who do have an existing WordPress.com account receive an email requesting them to click the **Accept Invitation** button.

WordPress notifies you by email when someone accepts an invitation.

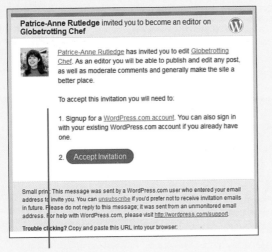

Invitee without a
WordPress.com account

Invitee with a
WordPress.com account

Manage Invitations

① From the main navigation menu, select **Users**, **Invite New**.

② In the Past Invitations section you can view the status of the invitations you sent.

③ Click **Resend** to send the invitation again.

④ Click **Delete** to delete an outstanding invitation that hasn't been accepted yet.

Did You Know?

You can't delete users who have accepted invitations on this screen. You must go to the Users screen to remove them. See "Remove a User" later in this chapter for more information.

Invitation accepted

Waiting for invitation to be accepted

Adding New Users (WordPress.org)

Add a New User

1. From the main navigation menu, select **Users, Add New**.

2. Enter basic information about your new users, such as a username, email address, first name, last name, and website.

   IMPORTANT *Although it isn't required, it's a good idea to add a first and last name for anyone who is going to create posts. For example, you want to display "Anne Smith" as the author of a post, not someone with the username "asmith82."*

3. Enter a password, twice.

4. If you want to send the password to your new user, select the **Send Password?** check box.

5. Select a user role from the drop-down list. Options include Administrator, Editor, Author, Contributor, or Subscriber.

6. Click the **Add New User** button.

7. WordPress displays the new user on the Users screen.

With self-hosted WordPress, you add new users one at a time on the Add New User screen.

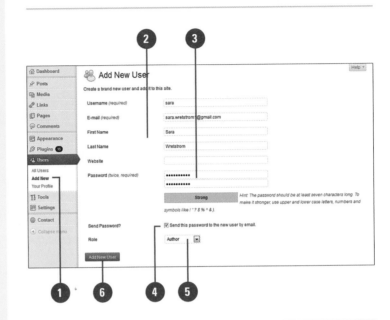

Did You Know?

The strength indicator lets you know how strong your password is. A good password should contain at least seven characters and include both uppercase and lowercase letters, numbers, and symbols (such as !, ?, and so forth).

Managing Your WordPress Users

On the Users screen, you can view and manage all your WordPress users in one place. On this screen, you can also remove or delete a user from your site or change a user's role, giving this person more or less access to your site.

View Users

1. From the main navigation menu, select **Users**, **All Users**.

2. By default, WordPress displays all users. Optionally, click a role link at the top of the screen to display only users for a specific role, such as Administrator or Author.

3. Click the **Username**, **Name**, or **E-mail** heading to sort users by this criteria.

4. Click the number in the **Posts** column to view all posts by this user.

5. Enter a user's name in the text box in the upper-right corner and click the **Search Users** button to find the right user in a long list.

6. Pause your mouse over a username and click the **Edit** link to edit this person's profile.

Did You Know?

WordPress.com refers to this action as removing, and self-hosted WordPress refers to it as deleting.) The result is the same.)

See Also

See Chapter 3, "Getting Started with WordPress.org," for more information about user profiles.

Remove a User (WordPress.com)

1. From the main navigation menu, select **Users**, **All Users**.

2. On the Users screen, pause your mouse over the user you want to remove and click the **Remove** link below this person's name.

3. On the Remove Users from Site screen, click the **Confirm Removal** button.

   TIMESAVER *Want to remove multiple users at once? Select the check box next to their names, select* **Remove** *from the Bulk Actions drop-down list, and click the* **Apply** *button.*

Did You Know?

WordPress.com doesn't delete the posts of a removed user or require you to assign posts to someone else. This person continues to display as the post author even after removal.

Remove Users from Site

You have specified these users for removal:

ID #45724370: sarawretstrom

Confirm Removal

Delete a User (WordPress.org)

1. From the main navigation menu, select **Users, All Users**.

2. On the Users screen, pause your mouse over the user you want to delete and click the **Delete** link below this person's name.

   TIMESAVER *Want to delete multiple users at once? Select the check box next to their names, select **Delete** from the Bulk Actions drop-down list, and click the **Apply** button.*

3. On the Delete Users screen, specify what to do with this person's posts, if anything: delete them or assign them to another user.

4. Click the **Confirm Deletion** button to permanently delete this user.

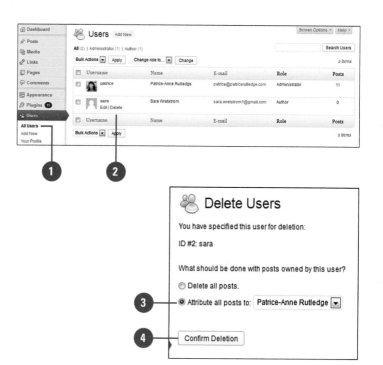

Change User Roles

1. From the main navigation menu, select **Users, All Users**.

2. Select the check box next to the name of the user (or users) whose role you want to change.

3. Select the new role from the **Change Role To** drop-down list.

4. Click the **Change** button.

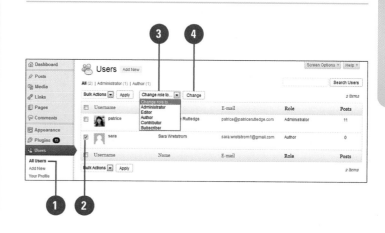

Did You Know?

You can also change a user's role on this person's individual profile (click the **Edit** link to open it). On this screen, you can also edit other user details including the password.

Managing Comments

Reader interaction is one the most important components of a successful blog—or the blog portion of a website. Fortunately, WordPress makes it easy to develop a community on your site with its powerful commenting tools.

Five Steps to Setting Up Your WordPress Commenting System

Following these five steps helps you make the most of the powerful commenting tools WordPress offers, enabling you to specify the exact features you want to use, encourage reader participation, and control spam.

1. On the Discussion Settings screen, specify how you want to manage comments on your website. There are many options on this screen, so take some time to read each one and decide how you want to handle that setting on your site. For example, you can specify your preferences on comment moderation and approval, email notifications, formatting, avatars, and so forth.

2. Decide whether you want to display comments, trackbacks, and pingbacks on your posts and pages. You specify this in the Discussion panel on the following screens: Add New/Edit Post or Add New/Edit Page. Your initial selection becomes the default for either posts or pages, but you can override this. In general, most WordPress users display comments on posts, but not on pages. You can also update this setting on a published post or page if you weren't aware of its significance when you first created it. See "Updating the Comments Setting on Existing Posts and Pages" later in this chapter.

See Also

See "Managing Discussion Settings" in Chapter 4, "Specifying WordPress Settings," for more information about the options on the Discussion Settings screen.

Did You Know?

As a reminder, trackbacks and pingbacks are a way of notifying web authors that you mentioned their content. For example, suppose you read a great post on another blog. You mention this post on your own blog, enter the URL of the original post in the Send Trackbacks panel, and WordPress displays this as a comment on the original post. If you mention a post on another WordPress site, WordPress handles notifications automatically via pingbacks.

See Also

See "Adding a Page" in Chapter 6, "Creating and Managing Pages," or "Creating a Post" in Chapter 7, "Creating and Managing Posts," for more information about allowing comments, trackbacks, and pingbacks.

3. Sign up for a Gravatar (http://en.gravatar.com) to display next to your comments on your own website as well as on other sites. A Gravatar, short for globally recognized avatar, is a small photo that represents you on the Web. You can specify how you want to use Gravatars and avatars on the Discussion Settings screen.

4. (WordPress.org) Activate the Akismet plugin to control spam. If you use WordPress.com, Akismet is activated by default. See "Activating the Akismet Plugin to Control Comment Spam (WordPress.org)" later in this chapter.

5. (WordPress.org) Optionally, select, install, and activate a commenting plug-in if you want more functionality than the standard WordPress commenting feature offers. Some popular plugins include Disqus, CommentLuv, Livefyre, and Triberr.

Did You Know?

If WordPress indicates that there is a new version of Akismet, you can upgrade to this version by clicking the **Update Now** link.

See Also

See "Commenting Plugins" in Appendix B, "WordPress Plugins (WordPress.org)," for more information about installing and using commenting plugins.

Activating the Akismet Plugin to Control Comment Spam (WordPress.org)

By default, WordPress installs the Akismet plugin (http://akismet.com) when you create your website. Although Akismet is optional, I highly recommend activating it to manage your comment spam automatically. The more popular your site becomes, the more attractive it is to spammers who submit irrelevant comments hoping to receive a link back to their own site if you approve their comments.

Activate the Akismet Plugin

1. On the main navigation menu, click **Plugins**.

    IMPORTANT *If you host your site with WordPress.com, Akismet manages your spam automatically; you don't need to install a plugin.*

2. Click the **Activate** link below the Akismet plugin.

3. Navigate to https://akismet.com/signup.

4. Select the option that best suits your site (Enterprise, Pro, or Personal) and click the **Sign Up** button.

Did You Know?

If WordPress indicates that there is a new version of Akismet, you can upgrade to this version by clicking the **Update Now** link.

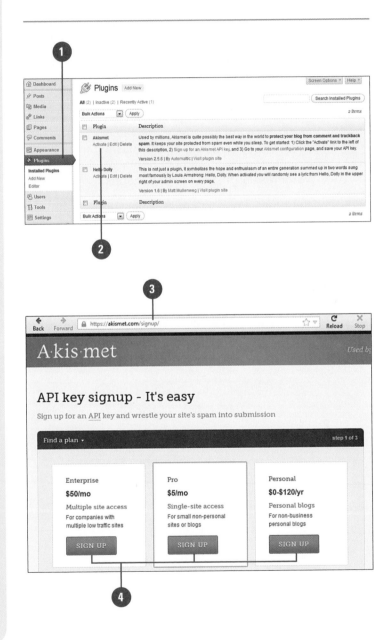

⑤ On the API Key Signup page, enter your name, email address, and payment information (if you selected a plan that requires payment).

⑥ Click the **Continue** button. Akismet sends you an email with your API key.

⑦ Return to WordPress and select **Plugins**, **Akismet Configuration** from the main navigation menu.

⑧ On the Akismet Configuration screen, enter the **Akismet API Key** you received in your email.

⑨ Optionally, select the **Auto-Delete Spam Submitted on Posts More Than a Month Old** check box to delete spam received on older posts.

⑩ Optionally, select the **Show the Number of Comments You've Approved Beside Each Comment Author** check box to display this number, which gives you a good idea of who is contributing valuable comments and who is not.

⑪ Click the **Update Options** button to activate Akismet.

How Akismet Works

Akismet monitors every comment your site receives and moves those it identifies as spam to your Spam folder. From there, you can decide whether each comment is actually spam. WordPress retains comments marked as spam in your Spam folder for 15 days and then deletes them if you take no action.

Akismet is free for personal sites, but requests a small payment from business sites. Self-hosted WordPress users need to sign up for a free API key to activate Akismet. API stands for Application Programming Interface, which enables WordPress to communicate with a third-party tool such as Akismet.

Updating the Comments Setting on Existing Posts and Pages

When you create a new post or page, you can specify whether you want to allow comments, trackbacks, or pingbacks in the Discussion panel on the Add New Post screen or the Add New Page screen. If you didn't do this, you can go back and change this setting for a specific post or page even after publishing.

Update the Comments Setting

1 On the main navigation menu, click **Posts** (or **Pages**).

2 Pause your mouse over the post or page you want to edit and click the **Quick Edit** link to open the Quick Edit section.

3 Select the **Allow Comments** check box to enable comments. If you don't want to allow comments, deselect this check box.

4 Select the **Allow Pings** check box to enable pingbacks and trackbacks. If you don't want to allow these, deselect this check box.

5 Click the **Update** button.

See Also

See "Adding a Page" in Chapter 6 or "Creating a Post" in Chapter 7 for more information about allowing comments, trackbacks, and pingbacks.

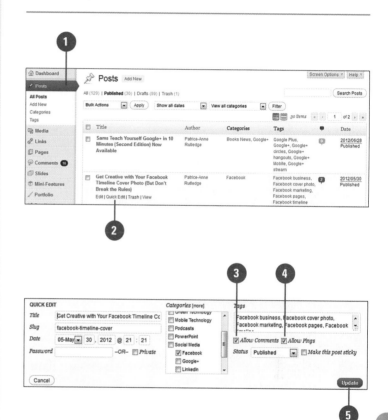

Moderating Comments

WordPress gives you complete control over comment moderation, enabling you to approve only the comments you want to display on your site. Deciding how you want to handle comment moderation is a personal choice. You can moderate comments on the Comments screen in WordPress or have WordPress email you whenever a new comment needs your attention. If you activated email comment notifications, WordPress sends you an email when someone posts a comment (based on your specifications on the Discussion Settings screen).

In addition, you can unapprove any comment if you approve it by mistake or change your mind about wanting to display it. You can also edit comments if you find errors in them.

View All Comments

1 On the main navigation menu, click **Comments**. The number of pending comments displays to the right of this menu option.

2 By default, WordPress displays all your comments, pingbacks, and trackbacks. Optionally, click one of the following links at the top of the screen to display only content that matches the selected status: **Pending**, **Approved**, or **Spam**.

3 Click the **Author** or **In Response To** (post) heading to sort your comments by this criteria.

4 If you want to filter the type of content that displays on the Comments screen, select either **Comments** or **Pings** from the Show All Comment Types drop-down list and click the **Filter** button. Separating actual comments from pingbacks can make it easier to review your site's commenting activity.

5 If you have a large number of comments, enter some text from the comment you want to find in the text box in the upper-right corner and click the **Search Comments** button.

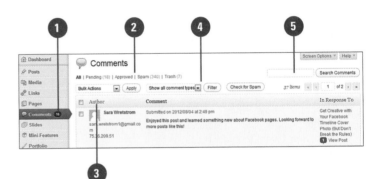

Did You Know?

On the Comments screen, you can view all your WordPress comments, pingbacks, and trackbacks in one place. If you have only a few, it's easy to review them. On the other hand, if your site contains numerous comments, WordPress offers several options for filtering, searching, and sorting to find exactly what you're looking for.

Approve a Comment

① On the main navigation menu, click **Comments**.

TIMESAVER Click the *Pending* link to display only comments pending approval.

② On the Comments screen, pause your mouse over the comment you want to approve and click the **Approve** link. WordPress approves the comment and displays it below the related post on your site.

Did You Know?

When you approve a comment, WordPress displays it on your site.

Unapprove a Comment

① On the main navigation menu, click **Comments**.

② On the Comments screen, pause your mouse over the comment you want to unapprove and click the **Unapprove** link. WordPress returns the comment to the Pending status and hides it from your site.

Reply to a Comment

1. On the main navigation menu, click **Comments**.

2. On the Comments screen, pause your mouse over the comment you want to reply to and click the **Reply** link to open the Reply to Comment section.

3. Enter your reply in the large text box.

4. Optionally, apply any formatting to your reply using the toolbar buttons. For example, you could apply bold or italic to your text, insert a link, or insert an image.

5. Click the **Reply** button. WordPress saves your reply and displays it on your site.

> **TIMESAVER** *You can also reply to a comment directly on your website by clicking the **Reply** button below a comment. See "Adding Comments to Your Own Site" later in this chapter.*

Did You Know?

Replying to the comments others leave on your site helps encourage participation and community. For example, you might want to answer a question or thank someone for his comment.

Did You Know?

If you selected the **Enable Threaded (Nested) Comments** check box on the Discussion Settings screen, WordPress indents your reply so readers know which comment you're responding to.

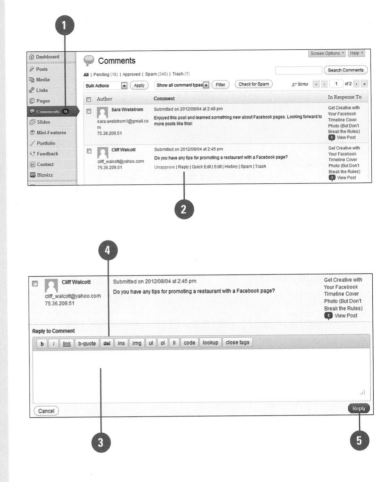

Edit a Comment

1. On the main navigation menu, click **Comments**.

2. On the Comments screen, pause your mouse over the comment you want to edit and click the **Quick Edit** link to open the Quick Edit section.

   IMPORTANT *You should reserve editing comments only for correcting true errors, such as a typo or broken link, or for removing private information such as phone numbers and email addresses. Never change the meaning of someone else's comment by adding or deleting content. If you don't like a comment, you don't need to display it on your site. A good practice when editing is to state that the comment has been edited. For example, if you remove an email address, you could add [email address redacted] to the comment.*

3. Make any changes to the comment.

4. Click the **Update Comment** button.

Did You Know?

Optionally, you can click the **Edit** link below a comment to edit the comment on the Edit Comment screen. The features on this screen are very similar to the Quick Edit box.

Respond to Email Comment Notifications

1 Open the comment notification email.

2 Take one of the following actions:

◆ If you want to approve the comment, click the **Approve It** link and then click the **Approve Comment** button on the Moderate Comment screen.

◆ If you want to delete the comment, click the **Trash It** link and then click the **Trash Comment** button on the Moderate Comment screen.

◆ If you want to mark the comment as spam, click the **Spam It** link and then click the **Spam Comment** button on the Moderate Comment screen.

A new comment on the post "Get Creative with Your Facebook Timeline Cover Photo (But Don't Break the Rules)" is waiting for your approval
http://patricerutledge.com/facebook-timeline-cover/

Author : Sara Wretstrom (IP: 75.36.209.51 , adsl-75-36-209-51.dsl.pltn13.sbcglobal.net)
E-mail : sara.wretstrom1@gmail.com
URL   :
Whois : http://whois.arin.net/rest/ip/75.36.209.51
Comment:
Enjoyed this post and learned something new about Facebook pages. Do you have any tips for promoting a restaurant with a Facebook page?

Approve it: http://patricerutledge.com/wp-admin/comment.php?action=approve&c=9779
Trash it: http://patricerutledge.com/wp-admin/comment.php?action=trash&c=9779
Spam it: http://patricerutledge.com/wp-admin/comment.php?action=spam&c=9779
Currently 31 comments are waiting for approval. Please visit the moderation panel:
http://patricerutledge.com/wp-admin/edit-comments.php?comment_status=moderated

2

Adding Comments to Your Own Site

Although your site visitors are more likely to comment on your website than you are, at times you might want to leave a comment on your own site. For example, you could respond to a reader comment or post additional or updated information you don't want to include in the post itself.

Add a Comment to Your Own Site

1. Log in to your WordPress site.

2. Navigate to the post you want to comment on.

3. Scroll down to the bottom of the page and enter your comment in the **Leave a Reply** section.

4. Click the **Post Comment** button.

> **IMPORTANT** *Depending on the theme you use, the exact wording and appearance of the comments section could vary, but the process is essentially the same.*

Did You Know?

If you want to reply to a specific comment rather than comment on the post itself, click the **Reply** button below that comment.

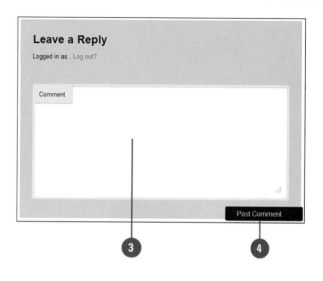

Deleting Comments

If you don't want to display specific comments on your website, you can delete them. As an extra precaution, WordPress makes you confirm deletion before removing comments permanently from your site. In case you delete by mistake, WordPress also lets you restore deleted comments.

Delete a Comment

1 On the main navigation menu, click **Comments**.

2 On the Comments screen, pause your mouse over the comment you want to delete and click the **Trash** link below it. WordPress moves the comment to the Trash folder.

> **TIMESAVER** *Want to delete multiple comments at once? Select the check box next to the comments you want to delete, select* **Move to Trash** *from the Bulk Actions drop-down list, and click the* **Apply** *button.*

> **IMPORTANT** *Did you delete a comment by mistake? Click the* **Undo** *link on the Comments screen to restore it immediately. This link is available only when you first delete a comment. If you want to restore a comment later, you can do so from the Trash folder.*

Restore a Deleted Comment

1. On the main navigation menu, click **Comments**.

2. Click the **Trash** link at the top of the Comments screen.

3. Pause your mouse over the comment you want to restore and click the **Restore** link. WordPress removes the comment from the Trash folder and restores it to the Comments screen as a pending comment.

Empty Comments from the Trash Folder

1. On the main navigation menu, click **Comments**.

2. Click the **Trash** link at the top of the Comments screen.

3. Click the **Empty Trash** button. WordPress deletes the comments permanently.

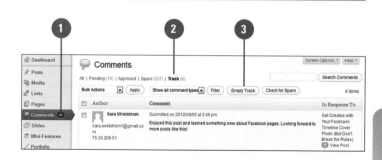

> **IMPORTANT** *If you want to delete only one comment permanently, pause your mouse over it and click the **Delete Permanently** link. Optionally, select the check boxes of multiple comments you want to empty from the Trash folder, select **Delete Permanently** from the Bulk Actions drop-down list, and click the **Apply** button.*

Managing Spam

Did You Know?

If you receive a lot of comment spam, consider using the Comment Moderation and Comment Blacklist features on the Discussion Settings screen. You can flag any comment for moderation that contain a specific number of links (spammers frequently add numerous comment links) or specific words (including email addresses). Blacklisting enables you to flag a comment directly as spam if it contains specific words.

Mark a Comment as Spam

① On the main navigation menu, click **Comments**.

② On the Comments screen, pause your mouse over the comment you want to mark as spam and click the **Spam** link. WordPress moves the comment to the Spam folder.

TIMESAVER *Do you want to mark multiple comments as spam at once? Select the check box next to the comments you want to mark, select **Mark as Spam** from the Bulk Actions drop-down list, and click the **Apply** button.*

Controlling spam is essential to the success of any website. Unfortunately, the more popular your site is, the more spam you'll have to control.

If you use WordPress.com, the Akismet feature moves suspected spam to your Spam folder automatically for you to review. If you use self-hosted WordPress, you can activate the Akismet plugin on the Plugins screen. See "Activating the Akismet Plugin to Control Comment Spam" earlier in this chapter for more information.

When you mark a comment as spam, WordPress notifies Akismet of this action. Akismet then takes this information into consideration when it analyzes future comments for spam.

If you discover a quality comment in the Spam folder, you can restore it. Doing this notifies Akismet, which takes this into consideration during future spam analysis. You can also restore comments you marked as spam by accident.

You can permanently remove the comments in the Spam folder by emptying it.

Restore a Comment Marked as Spam

1. On the main navigation menu, click **Comments**.

2. Click the **Spam** link at the top of the Comments screen.

3. Pause your mouse over the comment you want to restore and click the **Not Spam** link. WordPress removes the comment from the Spam folder and restores it to the Comments screen as a pending comment.

Empty Comments from the Spam Folder

1. On the main navigation menu, click **Comments**.

2. Click the **Spam** link at the top of the Comments screen.

3. Click the **Empty Spam** button. WordPress deletes the comments permanently.

IMPORTANT *If you want to delete only one comment permanently, pause your mouse over it and click the **Delete Permanently** link. Optionally, select the check boxes of multiple comments you want to empty from the Spam folder, select **Delete Permanently** from the Bulk Actions drop-down list, and click the **Apply** button.*

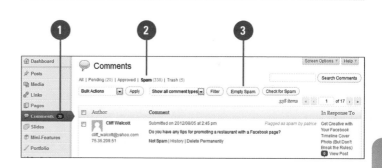

Managing Your
WordPress Website

Ensuring your website is backed up and secure is a critical part of managing a successful site. Keeping current with the latest version of any themes or plugins you use, as well as the current version of WordPress itself, is equally important. Finally, you also need an easy way to import, export, and delete your site if you no longer need it. Fortunately, Word-Press offers tools that simplify all these tasks.

Because the way you accomplish things differs between WordPress.com and self-hosted WordPress sites, this chapter is divided into two sections.

What You'll Do

Manage Your Website (WordPress.com)

Manage Your Website (WordPress.org)

Managing Your Website (WordPress.com)

One of the advantages of WordPress.com is it handles all your site backups for you; you don't need to install or do anything to ensure your content is secure. In addition, no action is required to update to a new version of WordPress. This also happens automatically.

Import Content into Your Website (WordPress.com)

1 From the main navigation menu, select **Tools**, **Import**.

2 On the Import screen, select the source of your existing content (this example uses WordPress).

Did You Know?

If you want to save your website content outside of WordPress.com's automated backups, you can export a copy of your website. See "Export Your Website Content" later in this chapter for more information.

Did You Know?

If you have an existing website, you can import your content into your new WordPress site without manual data entry. WordPress enables you to import content from numerous sources, including other WordPress sites, Blogger, Israblog, OPML, Live-Journal, Moveable Type, Typepad, Posterous, Splinder, Tumblr, and Yahoo! 360.

On the Import WordPress screen, click the **Browse** button.

IMPORTANT *The specific steps for importing vary depending on the source of your content.*

Select the file you want to import and click **Open**. (The exact name of this dialog box and button vary by operating system and browser).

IMPORTANT *The maximum file size you can import is 15MB.*

Click the **Upload File and Import** button.

Specify how you want to assign imported content to existing authors by selecting a name from the drop-down list.

Click the **Submit** button to start the import process.

Did You Know?

If you're importing content from another WordPress site, see "Export Your Website Content" for more information about exporting the content you want to import into your new site. If you're importing content from another system, refer to its instructions for exporting.

Did You Know?

The time it takes to complete this process depends on the amount of content you're importing. WordPress sends you an email when it's finished importing. When you receive this notification, you can view your imported content on WordPress, such as on the Posts, Pages, Categories, and Tags screens.

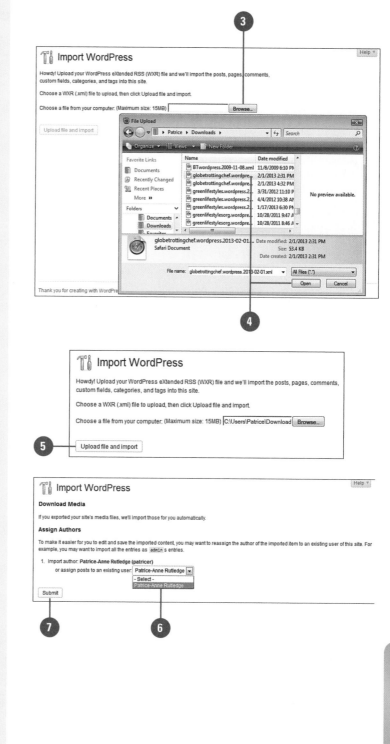

Export Your Website Content

① From the main navigation menu, select **Tools**, **Export**.

② Click **Export**.

> **TIMESAVER** *Selecting the* ***Guided Transfer*** *option enables you to easily move your WordPress.com website to a self-hosted WordPress site with the assistance of trained engineers for $129.*

③ Select what you want to export, such as All Content, Posts, Pages, or Feedbacks.

> **IMPORTANT** *Unless you have a strong reason for exporting only a portion of your WordPress content, you should select **All Content**.*

④ Click the **Download Export File** button.

⑤ In the dialog box that opens, select **Save File** and click **OK**. WordPress downloads your file to your default download directory.

Did You Know?

Exporting your WordPress site is useful if you want to make an extra backup of your content or you're planning to move it to a new site or system. When you export, WordPress creates an XML file that contains your site content. The file-naming convention includes the name of your site and the current date, such as globetrottingchef. wordpress.2013-02-02.xml.

See Also

See Chapter 15, "Using WordPress. com Premium Features," for more information about purchasing a guided transfer.

Delete Your Website

IMPORTANT *If you think you might want to reuse your site content again, export a copy of it. See "Export Your Website Content" earlier in this chapter.*

1. From the main navigation menu, select **Tools**, **Delete Blog**.

2. On the Delete Blog screen, select the goal for deleting your blog (in this case, you should select **Permanently Delete the Blog Name and All Content**).

3. Click the check box that indicates you understand this is a permanent, irreversible action.

4. Optionally, enter an explanation about why you're deleting your site.

5. Click the **Delete [*website name*] Permanently** button. The name of this button varies based on the name of your site.

IMPORTANT *WordPress sends you an email verifying you really want to delete your site. You must click this link to finalize the deletion.*

Did You Know?

If you decide you no longer need your WordPress.com website, you can delete it. Depending on your reason for deletion, WordPress offers recommendations and suggestions for alternatives. For example, if you indicate you want to delete your site so you can move it to another host, WordPress suggested its Guided Transfer and Offsite Redirect upgrades. In this example, you delete your blog and all content permanently.

For Your Information

WordPress.com Deletion Goals

WordPress requires you to select a goal for deleting your website to help you make the right choice and avoid a costly or irreversible mistake. Your options include the following:

- ◆ Change My Blog's URL
- ◆ Transfer My Blog to Another User
- ◆ Move to Another Host
- ◆ Empty My Blog of All Content
- ◆ Free Up the Blog Name So Somebody Else Can Use It
- ◆ Permanently Delete the Blog Name and All Content

Managing Your Website (WordPress.org)

Managing your self-hosted WordPress website requires you to be proactive about important tasks such as backing up and updating your site.

The process for backing up varies greatly depending on which plugin you use, what you want to back up, and where you want to store your backup. In this example, you back up your site to the server using the BackWPup plugin default settings. You must install this plugin to see the BackWPup options on your WordPress menu. The actual steps differ if you use another plugin, but the concept is the same.

Back Up Your Website

1 From the main navigation menu, select **BackWPup**, **Add New**.

2 Enter a name for your backup.

3 Select the **Activate Scheduling** check box to activate the default daily backup schedule.

4 In the Backup to Folder section, enter the folder path where you want to store your backups. WordPress provides a sample folder structure based on your website.

5 Indicate the maximum number of backups you want to store. For example, you might want to keep at least three backup files in case

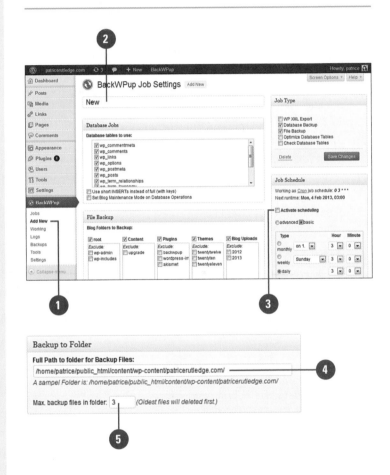

something goes wrong.

6 Click the **Save Changes** button.

IMPORTANT *Remember to verify that your backup actually is in the location you specified, such as on the server, on Dropbox, and so forth.*

Did You Know?

You can view your scheduled backup on the BackWPup Jobs screen (select **BackWPup**, **Jobs**). To run a backup immediately rather than waiting for the next scheduled backup, pause your mouse over the job and click the **Run Now** link.

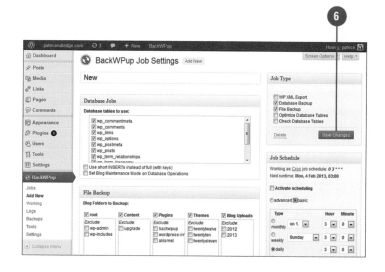

Backup in progress

WordPress Backup Plugins

Backing up your website is a critical task. Fortunately, you can install several plugins that simplify the backup process. Here are three good backup plugins to consider:

◆ **BackWPup** (http://wordpress.org/extend/plugins/backwpup)—Back up in a variety of formats (such as .zip and .tar) to your computer, an FTP server, Amazon S3, Google Storage, Microsoft Azure, Rackspace Cloud, Dropbox, SugarSync, or email.

◆ **Backup Buddy** (http://ithemes.com/purchase/backupbuddy)—Premium plugin, with pricing starting at $75, that enables you to download backups to your desktop or send them to Dropbox, Amazon S3, Rackspace Cloud, an FTP server, or an email address.

◆ **WordPress Backup to Dropbox** (http://wordpress.org/extend/plugins/wordpress-backup-to-dropbox)—Back up to your Dropbox account.

Install WordPress Updates (WordPress.org)

IMPORTANT *Be sure to back up your data before installing updates. Although most updates install without any problems, it is possible to encounter a conflict. See "Back Up Your Website" earlier in this chapter for more information.*

1 From the main navigation menu, select **Dashboard**, **Updates**.

2 Click the **Update Now** button to update to a new version of WordPress.

Did You Know?

WordPress continually delivers updates that add new functionality, fix bugs, and resolve security issues. In addition, plugins and themes often have updates. When a new version of WordPress is available, a notification displays at the top of the screen. You can also view and install all updates on the WordPress Updates screen.

Did You Know?

You might not see all these update options on the WordPress Updates screen if your system is already updated.

Four updates available

Learn about new WordPress version

One plugin update available

Update to new version

Check for new updates

Learn more about new update

IMPORTANT *Although the WordPress Updates screen makes it easy to perform all your updates in one place, you should check your website thoroughly after each update before proceeding to the next. For example, if you update WordPress, five plugins, and your theme and then discover your website no longer displays correctly, it would take more time to figure out which update caused the problem. By performing them one at a time, you can verify that everything is working okay before installing another update.*

3 Select the check box next to a plugin you want to update and click the **Update Plugins** button.

4 Select the check box next to a theme you want to update and click the **Update Themes** button.

Plugins

The following plugins have new versions available. Check the ones you want to update and then click "Update Plugins".

[Update Plugins]

☐ Select All

☐ **Akismet**
    You have version 2.5.3 installed. Update to 2.5.7. View version 2.5.7 details.
    Compatibility with WordPress 3.5.1: 100% (according to its author)

☐ Select All

[Update Plugins]

Themes

The following themes have new versions available. Check the ones you want to update and then click "Update Themes".

Please Note: Any customizations you have made to theme files will be lost. Please consider using child themes for modifications.

[Update Themes]

☐ Select All

☐ **Twenty Eleven**
    You have version 1.3 installed. Update to 1.5.

☐ **Twenty Ten**
    You have version 1.3 installed. Update to 1.5.

Import Content Into Your Website

1. From the main navigation menu, select **Tools**, **Import**.

   IMPORTANT *If you have an existing website, you can import your content (such as pages, posts, categories, and media) into your new WordPress site without manual data entry.*

2. On the Import screen, select the source of your existing content (in this case, click **WordPress**).

3. Click the **Install Now** button to install the WordPress Importer plugin.

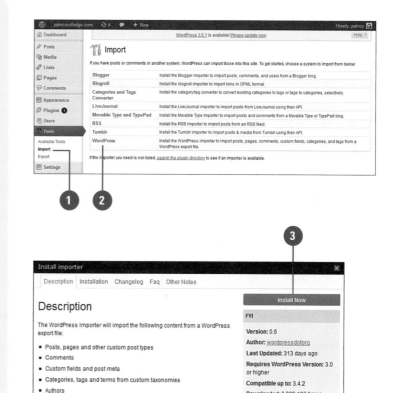

Did You Know?

If you're importing content from another WordPress site, see "Export Your Website Content" for more information about how to export the content you want to import into your new site. If you're importing content from another system, refer to its instructions for exporting.

Did You Know?

WordPress enables you to import content from numerous sources, including other WordPress sites, Blogger, OPML, LiveJournal, Moveable Type, Typepad, and Tumblr.

For Your Information

From WordPress.com to WordPress.org

If you decide to move your content from WordPress.com to a self-hosted WordPress website, you can do so quickly by exporting and then importing your content. This technique, however, is most useful for sites with only a small amount of content and limited traffic. If you've been blogging on WordPress.com for a while and have developed a significant amount of content and a solid audience, you should consider purchasing the Guided Transfer and Site Redirect upgrades, which provide support from trained engineers and enable you to retain traffic and search engine rankings from your previous site. For more information, see Chapter 15.

4 Click the **Activate Plugin & Run Importer** link.

5 On the Import WordPress screen, click the **Browse** button.

IMPORTANT *The specific steps for importing vary depending on the source of your content.*

6 Select the file you want to import and click **Open**. (The exact name of this dialog box and button varies by operating system and browser).

Did You Know?

If you've already installed the WordPress Importer plugin, you skip steps 3 and 4.

Did You Know?

If an importer for your source content doesn't display on the Import screen, click the **Search the Plugin Directory** link to find other importer plugins you can install and use.

Installing Plugin: WordPress Importer 0.6

Downloading install package from http://downloads.wordpress.org/plugin/wordpress-importer.0.6.zip...

Unpacking the package...

Installing the plugin...

Successfully installed the plugin **WordPress Importer 0.6**.

Activate Plugin & Run Importer | Return to Importers

Import WordPress

Howdy! Upload your WordPress eXtended RSS (WXR) file and we'll import the posts, pages, comments, custom fields, categories, and tags into this site.

Choose a WXR (.xml) file to upload, then click Upload file and import.

Choose a file from your computer: (Maximum size: 64MB) [   ] Browse...

Upload file and import

File Upload

Patrice ▸ Downloads ▸   ▾ | ✦ | Search

Organize ▾ | Views ▾ | New Folder

Favorite Links	Name	Date modified
Documents	BTwordpress.2009-11-08.xml	11/8/2009 6:10 PM
Recently Changed	globetrottingchef.wordpre...	2/1/2013 2:31 PM
Recent Places	globetrottingchef.wordpre...	2/1/2013 4:32 PM
More »	greenlifestyles.wordpress.2...	3/31/2012 11:10 P
	greenlifestyles.wordpress.2...	4/4/2012 10:38 AM
Folders	greenlifestyles.wordpress.2...	1/17/2013 6:30 PM
Documents	greenlifestylesorg.wordpre...	10/28/2011 9:47 A
Downloads	greenlifestylesorg.wordpre...	10/28/2011 8:46 A

No preview available.

globetrottingchef.wordpress.2013-02-01...   Date modified: 2/1/2013 2:31 PM
Safari Document   Size: 53.4 KB
                                           Date created: 2/1/2013 2:31 PM

File name: globetrottingchef.wordpress.2013-02-01.xml ▾   All Files (*.*) ▾

Open   Cancel

Thank you for creating with WordPre

7 Click the **Upload File and Import** button.

8 Specify how you want to assign imported content to existing authors by selecting a name from the drop-down list.

9 Click the **Download and Import File Attachments** check box if your source file includes media attachments and you want to import them.

10 Click the **Submit** button to import the file.

Did You Know?

Optionally, you can create a new user to assign to your posts. Another option is to download and import file attachments.

🍶 Import WordPress

Howdy! Upload your WordPress eXtended RSS (WXR) file and we'll import the posts, pages, comments, custom fields, categories, and tags into this site.

Choose a WXR (.xml) file to upload, then click Upload file and import.

Choose a file from your computer: (Maximum size: 64MB) [C:\Users\Patrice\Download] [Browse..]

[Upload file and import]

7

9

Create new user

🍶 Import WordPress

Assign Authors

To make it easier for you to edit and save the imported content, you may want to reassign the author of the imported item to an existing user of this site. For example, you may want to import all the entries as admin's entries.

If a new user is created by WordPress, a new password will be randomly generated and the new user's role will be set as subscriber. Manually changing the new user's details will be necessary.

Import author: Patrice-Anne Rutledge (patricer)
or create new user with login name: [   ]
or assign posts to an existing user: patrice [▾]

Import Attachments

☐ Download and import file attachments

[Submit]

10   **8**

Export Your Website Content

1. From the main navigation menu, select **Tools**, **Export**.

2. Select what you want to export, such as All Content, Posts, or Pages.

   IMPORTANT *Unless you have a strong reason for exporting only a portion of your WordPress content, you should select* ***All Content***.

3. Click the **Download Export File** button.

4. In the dialog box that opens, select **Save File** and click **OK**. WordPress downloads your file to your default download directory.

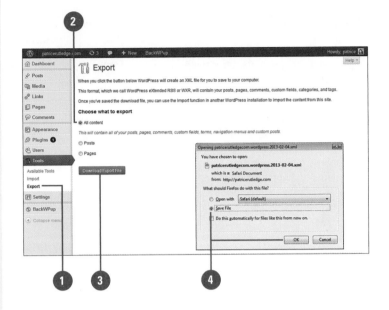

Did You Know?

Exporting your WordPress site is useful if you want to make an extra backup of your content or if you're planning to move it to a new site or system. When you export, WordPress creates an XML file that contains your site content. The file-naming convention includes the name of your site and the current date, such as patricerutledgecom. wordpress.2013-02-03.xml

Deleting a Self-Hosted WordPress Website

If you're familiar with WordPress.com, you might be aware that it offers an automated site-deletion tool. Self-hosted WordPress sites don't include this feature. Instead, you need to delete your website through your web host or via FTP. If you're unsure how to do this, contact your web host directly.

For WordPress sites installed using cPanel, for example, there is a Remove link to the right of every WordPress install that enables you to delete it permanently.

If you want to delete all your content (posts, pages, categories, images, and so forth), but retain the website itself, consider the Empty WP Blog/Website plugin (http://wordpress.org/extend/plugins/empty-wp-blog-or-website).

If want to reuse any of your website content in the future, be sure to back it up.

Click to delete site

WordPress Premium Themes

Choosing a WordPress premium theme can make a big difference in the quality of your site, providing additional features and functionality, professional design, and critical support and updates. In this appendix, I suggest some good sources for premium themes, including several I've used on my own WordPress sites.

See Also

See Chapter 5, "Working with Themes," to learn how to choose, install, and customize a theme.

IMPORTANT *If you use WordPress.com, you can't download and install a premium theme. Instead, search for premium themes on the Manage Themes screen on your WordPress.com site. Although some of the themes mentioned in this chapter are available on WordPress.com, not all are.*

Woo Themes

Woo Themes (www.woothemes.com) offers a collection of themes suited to business, e-commerce, magazines, portfolios, and personal blogs. All Woo themes run on the Woo framework, which includes built-in search engine optimization (SEO), custom navigation, a sidebar manager, and custom shortcodes (ideal for adding buttons, boxes, and columns with no coding). If you plan to sell from your site, you might be interested in the free WooCommerce plugin that adds e-commerce functionality.

Theme pricing begins at $70 for three themes with lifetime support. Another option is the Club Subscription ($125 startup fee plus $20 per month), suited to designers and developers who want access to all Woo themes. Woo also offers several of its older themes at no charge. If you want to try before you buy, go to the Theme Playground (test.woothemes.com), where you can get free hands-on experience working with all the themes Woo offers.

StudioPress

StudioPress (www.studiopress.com) runs all its themes off the Genesis framework, a fully customizable development tool that works with StudioPress's many child themes. These child themes include those suited for real estate agents, magazines, agencies, lifestyle sites, crafts, and weddings. StudioPress also offers many plugins that enhance and extend the functionality of its themes with social networking, e-commerce, sliders, and more. If you're overwhelmed with the choices available, check out the Theme Chooser (www.studiopress.com/choose-theme), which helps you narrow your options by category and layout.

Pricing begins at $99.95 for a single theme plus the Genesis framework with unlimited updates, sites, and support. Discounts are available if you need only the framework or if you already own the framework and just want another theme. If you're a developer, consider the Pro Plus Package, which gives you access to all themes for $349.95.

Thesis

Thesis (diythemes.com) offers a solid framework for building a WordPress site. Thesis doesn't provide child themes or ready-made designs; instead, it's a flexible development framework that lets you customize the exact layout and design you want for your site. Thesis is known for its search engine optimization features, fast load times, and typography control.

Experienced WordPress users enjoy Thesis for its power and flexibility, but new users could be a bit overwhelmed if they aren't willing to invest in the learning curve required to master it. Thesis is priced at $87 for use on one website with lifetime updates or $164 for the developer's options, which gives you the right to use Thesis on multiple sites.

Headway

Headway (www.headwaythemes.com) offers a drag-and-drop visual framework that you can use to design a precise WordPress theme with the exact fonts, colors, and styles you want to use. Headway Extend enables you to extend Headway with predesigned themes or blocks (layout elements such as sliders, tabs, galleries, and so forth). If you want to give Headway a test drive, you can do so at demo. headwaythemes.com.

Headway is priced at $87 for unlimited use or $174 for the developer option that also includes four Headway Extend credits and early beta access to major theme updates. These prices include access to support, updates, and documentation for one year. If you require further updates or support, you can renew for 25 percent of the original price you paid.

Solostream

Solostream (www.solostream.com) offers a variety of easy-to-customize WordPress themes, with sliders, custom widgets, and multiple layout options.

Theme pricing begins at $59, but the Solostream Premium Themes Membership starting at $79 per month is a better deal if you want more than one theme. With this plan, you can receive unlimited use rights to all premium themes. Solostream also offers several free WordPress themes for the price challenged, as well as custom WordPress design for those with a larger budget.

Templatic

Templatic (www.templatic.com) offers a solid collection of themes suitable for business sites, portfolios, online stores, magazines, and multimedia sites. The Templatic collection also includes many industry themes for schools, hotels, real estate agents, spas, lawyers, musicians, authors, and more. If you would like to try out Templatic themes, you can create a free test site at http://test.templatic.com.

Templatic themes are priced at $65 for a single-domain license with support and updates for one year. For $99, you can use the theme on multiple domains and receive the design source file (PSD files). Developers might be interested in the Premium Themes Club, priced at $299 for the first month and then $15 per month for access to all themes and all PSDs. The budget challenged should check out Templatic's free themes at templatic.com/category/freethemes.

Even More Themes

Still want to explore a few more options? Here are several other sources for high-quality premium themes:

- ◆ **Elegant Themes**
  (www.elegantthemes.com) —
  Charges $39 for complete access to every theme in their collection, currently totaling 77 themes. The developer version, priced at $89, gives you access to PSD files as well.

- ◆ **App Themes**
  (www.appthemes.com) —
  Offers application-based WordPress themes for functions such as job listings, coupon management, classified ads, issue tracking, or a business directory. Each theme costs $99.

- ◆ **WPMU DEV** (http://premium.wpmudev.org/projects/category/themes/) — A collection of premium themes; many work with the social networking plugin BuddyPress. Pricing begins at $39 per theme.

> **Did You Know?**
>
> Many premium theme developers showcase sites developed using their themes. This is a great source of ideas and inspiration for how you could use or customize a theme you're considering.

IMPORTANT *Before choosing a premium theme, assess your technical skills. Some themes require limited technical knowledge and are designed for the average person to use with limited customization. Others, however, provide extensive flexibility but require a reasonable level of technical savvy. Premium themes such as Thesis and Headway fall into this category.*

WordPress Plugins (WordPress.org)

Plugins can take your WordPress.org website from ordinary to extraordinary with a variety of content enhancements. Behind the scenes, plugins can simplify, streamline, and secure the process of managing your site. With thousands of plugins to choose from, the main challenge is choosing the right ones for your site.

In this appendix, I offer a roundup of my favorite plugins, including many that I use on my own WordPress sites. Unless otherwise noted, these plugins are free.

See Also

See Chapter 12, "Working with Plugins (WordPress.org)" for more information about finding, installing, and managing WordPress.org plugins.

See Also

See Appendix C, "Going Mobile with WordPress," to learn about mobile plugins and apps.

Backup Plugins

Backing up your website and its content is a critical task in WordPress. Here are several good options that ensure your site content is safe and secure.

- **Backup Buddy** (http://pluginbuddy.com/purchase/backupbuddy/)—Back up WordPress with options to download to your computer, email your backup, or send to Dropbox, Amazon S3, Rackspace Cloud, or other online storage sites. Premium plugin with pricing starting at $75.

- **BackWPUp** (http://wordpress.org/extend/plugins/backwpup/)—Back up WordPress to an FTP server, an email account, S3, Dropbox, SugarSync, Rackspace Cloud, and more.

- **WP-DB-Backup** (http://wordpress.org/extend/plugins/wp-db-backup/)—Back up your WordPress database on demand.

Commenting and Community

Although WordPress comes with its own commenting system, you should consider using one of these powerful plugins if you have an active community with lots of comments.

- **Comment Redirect** (http://wordpress.org/extend/plugins/comment-redirect/)—Redirect first-time commenters to a specific page on your site, such as an invitation to subscribe to your blog, like you on Facebook, or take another action.

- **CommentLuv** (http://wordpress.org/extend/plugins/commentluv/)—Increase your site comments by rewarding commenters with a link to their latest post.

- **Disqus Comment System** (http://wordpress.org/extend/plugins/disqus-comment-system/)—Enhance your site's commenting functionality with search engine optimization (SEO) indexing, threaded commenting, and connection to the Disqus community (which can increase your exposure and readership).

E-commerce Plugins

Do you want to sell online? Here are options for every budget.

- **MarketPress** (http://wordpress.org/extend/plugins/wordpress-ecommerce/)—Create an online store on your site. MarketPress Lite is free and offers basic e-commerce functionality. The paid version, priced at $39, supports digital downloads, multiple payment gateways, and coupons.

- **Pay per View** (http://premium.wpmudev.org/project/pay-per-view/) — Receive payments using the pay-per-view model. Premium theme priced at $39.

- **WooCommerce** (http://wordpress.org/extend/plugins/woocommerce/) — Create an online store on any WordPress site (but works particularly well with an accompanying WooCommerce theme). Features include multiple payment gateways, support for physical and digital products, shipping options, Google Analytics integration, social sharing, and coupons. Also offers a variety of fee-based extensions that provide even more e-commerce features and flexibility.

Media Plugins

Media plugins enable you to create dazzling image galleries and slideshows, integrate podcasts and videos, and more.

- **Blubrry PowerPress** (http://wordpress.org/extend/plugins/powerpress/) — Integrate podcasting on your WordPress site, including iTunes support and media players.

- **NextGEN Gallery** (http://wordpress.org/extend/plugins/nextgen-gallery/) — Create customizable image galleries, including slideshows and thumbnail galleries.

- **SlideDeck 2 Lite Content Slider** (http://wordpress.org/extend/plugins/slidedeck-lite-for-wordpress/) — Create an easy slider without code using your own images and text as well as content from YouTube, Flickr, and Pinterest.

Membership Plugins

WordPress offers several options for creating membership sites, which are a popular and profitable way to create an online community.

- **aMember Professional** (http://www.amember.com/p/) — Create a membership site with features including unlimited membership levels, incremental content delivery, coupon codes, and an affiliate panel. aMember Professional is priced at $179.95.

- **Membership** (http://wordpress.org/extend/plugins/membership/) — Create a basic membership site with this free plugin. Also offers a Pro version, priced at $39, which offers additional features, including BuddyPress integration.

- **Paid Memberships Pro** (http://wordpress.org/extend/plugins/paid-memberships-pro/)—A free membership plugin that integrates with Authorize.net or PayPal.

- **WishList Member** (http://member.wishlistproducts.com/)—Create a membership site with numerous features and options, including membership levels, multilevel access, shopping cart integration, controlled content viewing, flexible membership options, and more. Premium pricing starts at $97 for one domain and $297 for a multisite license for unlimited domains.

Security Plugins

Protecting your WordPress site from hackers should be a priority. Fortunately, you don't need to understand every security acronym to avoid attackers and intrusions with these easy-to-use plugins.

- **Better WP Security** (http://wordpress.org/extend/plugins/better-wp-security/)—Protect your website with one-click activation for most features, with the option for customization if you have advanced security knowledge.

- **Bulletproof Security** (http://wordpress.org/extend/plugins/bulletproof-security/)—Protect your website against hackers, including XSS, RFI, CRLF, CSRF, Base64, code injection, and SQL injection hacking.

SEO Plugins

Creating quality content on your WordPress site doesn't do much good if potential readers can't find it. These plugins help you optimize your content for search engines, create sitemaps that make your content easier to find, and analyze the results.

- **Google Analytics for WordPress** (http://wordpress.org/extend/plugins/google-analytics-for-wordpress/)—Track your WordPress site activity with Google Analytics, including views per page, views per author and category, and outbound clicks.

- **Google XML Sitemaps** (http://wordpress.org/extend/plugins/google-sitemap-generator/)—Generate a sitemap that helps search engines to index your site.

- **Google XML Sitemaps for Images** (http://wordpress.org/extend/plugins/google-image-sitemap/)—Generate a sitemap for your website images.

- **Google XML Sitemaps for Video** (http://wordpress.org/extend/plugins/xml-sitemaps-for-videos/)—Generate a sitemap for your video content.

- **WordPress SEO by Yoast** (http://wordpress.org/extend/plugins/wordpress-seo/)—Optimize your site for search engines, including features that help you create better titles, block duplicate pages, and more. This option eliminates the need for Google sitemaps plugins.

Social Plugins

Social sharing is an important part of growing your website's traffic and audience. Here are several plugins that help encourage social sharing and discovery.

- **Facebook for WordPress** (http://wordpress.org/extend/plugins/facebook/)—Integrate your site with Facebook, including the capability to share your content directly to your Facebook page or profile, mention friends and pages in your posts, and more. This plugin is powerful but best suited to users with strong technical skills.

- **Pinterest Pinboard Widget** (http://wordpress.org/extend/plugins/pinterest-pinboard-widget/)—Display your Pinterest pins on an attractive sidebar widget.

- **AddThis** (http://www.addthis.com/)—Enable site visitors to share your content on more than 120 sites, including Twitter, Facebook, LinkedIn, Google+, Pinterest, and other social sites. This plugin offers multiple display formats and customization options.

- **Sociable** (http://wordpress.org/extend/plugins/sociable/)—Add icons to your posts, encouraging readers to share your content on Twitter, Facebook, LinkedIn, Google+, and other social sites. Sociable includes options for both the classic button display at the end of a post and a vertical skyscraper display.

- **Social Media Widget** (http://wordpress.org/extend/plugins/social-media-widget/)—Display a sidebar widget with icons leading to your favorite social profiles. This widget includes several customization options and supports dozens of social sites, including Twitter, Facebook, LinkedIn, Google+, Pinterest, YouTube, Tumblr, and SlideShare.

Utility Plugins

This collection of plugins works behind the scenes to help you manage your site efficiently.

- **Broken Link Checker** (http://wordpress.org/extend/plugins/broken-link-checker/)—Monitor your site for broken links.

- **JetPack** (http://wordpress.org/extend/plugins/jetpack/)—Enhance your WordPress website with features available only on WordPress.com, including on-site statistics, the WP.me URL shortener, hovercard pop-ups for your Gravatar, a recent tweets widget, photo galleries, and more.

- **Private Only** (http://wordpress.org/extend/plugins/private-only/)—Create a private website that requires users to log in. This plugin is also useful for websites under development that aren't ready for public viewing.

- **Revision Control** (http://wordpress.org/extend/plugins/revision-control/)—Control the number of revisions that are saved for each post or page, keeping your site fast and lean.

- **W3 Total Cache** (http://wordpress.org/extend/plugins/w3-total-cache/)—Load your WordPress pages faster.

- **WordPress Importer** (http://wordpress.org/extend/plugins/wordpress-importer/)—Import posts, pages, comments, categories, tags, and more from an exported WordPress file.

The Best of the Rest

Here's a roundup of other great plugins that don't fit into any of the previous categories.

- **bbPress** (http://wordpress.org/extend/plugins/bbpress/)—Add a forum to your site.

- **BuddyPress** (http://wordpress.org/extend/plugins/buddypress/)—Create a social network on your site that includes profiles, messaging, and groups. More than 300 additional plugins are available to extend the functionality of BuddyPress. This plugin requires technical skill and isn't for beginners.

- **Contact Form 7** (http://wordpress.org/extend/plugins/contact-form-7/)—Display a customizable contact form on your website.

- **Editorial Calendar** (http://wordpress.org/extend/plugins/editorial-calendar/)—Manage your site content using this drag-and-drop post management tool.

- **Gravity Forms** (http://www.gravityforms.com/)—Create fully customizable forms, including order forms, multipage forms, and more. Priced at $39.

- **PollDaddy Polls and Ratings** (http://wordpress.org/extend/plugins/polldaddy/)—Create, display, and manage user polls within WordPress.

- **The Events Calendar** (http://wordpress.org/extend/plugins/the-events-calendar/)—Add a customizable events calendar, including Google Maps integration.

◆ **WP-PageNavi** (http://wordpress.org/extend/plugins/wp-pagenavi/)—
Enhance the default WordPress page navigation.

◆ **Yet Another Related Posts Plugin** (http://wordpress.org/extend/plugins/
yet-another-related-posts-plugin/)—Display related posts at the end of your
blog posts, encouraging readers to stay on your site.

Going Mobile with WordPress

WordPress makes it easy to update your site on the go with mobile apps designed for many popular smartphones and tablets. Although these apps don't enable you to access every WordPress feature, you can post, upload photos, and manage comments wherever you are.

In addition to updating your own WordPress site from a mobile device, you need to ensure that your readers are able to view your site easily on their mobile devices as well. The number of users who access the Web via mobile is growing, and offering them a viewing experience specifically designed for mobile helps to expand and retain your audience.

WordPress Mobile Apps

WordPress offers several free apps for posting on the go from your mobile device. Although the exact features of each app vary, most enable you to post and edit content, upload photos, and manage comments.

- ◆ **WordPress for iOS** (http://ios.wordpress.org)—Supports the iPhone, iPod Touch, and iPad.

- ◆ **WordPress for Android 2.0** (http://android.wordpress.org)—Supports Android devices running version 2.1 or later, including tablets.

- ◆ **WordPress for BlackBerry** (http://blackberry.wordpress.org).

- ◆ **WordPress for Windows Phone** (http://windowsphone.wordpress.org).

- ◆ **WordPress for Nokia** (http://nokia.wordpress.org)—Supports the S60 or Maemo-powered Nokia.

- ◆ **WordPress for webOS** (http://webos.wordpress.org)—Supports the HP TouchPad.

> ### Did You Know?
>
> If you don't have a phone or tablet that works with one of these apps, you can also access WordPress.com at m.wordpress.com. Be aware that this mobile version contains fewer features than an app designed for a specific device.

Use QuickPhoto to quickly upload photos from your iPhone

Update WordPress from your Android tablet

WordPress.com Mobile Theme

By default, WordPress.com comes with an enabled mobile theme. This mobile theme works with your installed theme (such as the default, Twenty Twelve) and is designed to load quickly and display well on a small screen.

Twenty Twelve offers a responsive layout, which adapts to the screen size on which your site is viewed, whether that's a desktop computer, notebook computer, tablet, or smartphone. To find similar themes, select the Responsive Layout check box on the Manage Themes page when searching for themes (select **Appearance**, **Themes** from the menu). You can also view suitable themes at http://theme.wordpress.com/themes/features/responsive-width.

If your preferred theme doesn't have a responsive layout, WordPress.com displays the Minileven theme (modified from the Twenty Eleven theme) for mobile viewers.

You can disable the WordPress.com mobile theme or specify how you want to handle excerpts on the Mobile Options screen (select **Appearance**, **Mobile** from the menu).

IMPORTANT *Unless you have a specific reason for disabling the mobile theme, you should leave it enabled.*

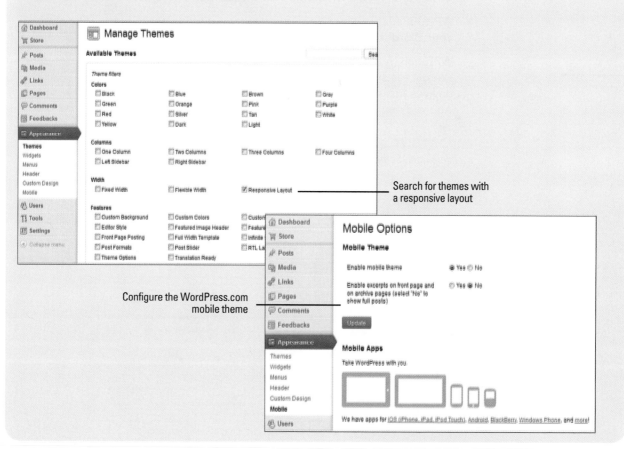

Search for themes with a responsive layout

Configure the WordPress.com mobile theme

Mobile Plugins (WordPress.org)

If your self-hosted WordPress website doesn't have a responsive theme or doesn't display well on mobile devices, installing a mobile plugin is a good way to resolve this problem. Make your site mobile-ready with these easy-to-use plugins.

See Also

See Chapter 12, "Working with Plugins (WordPress.org)," for more information about finding, installing, and managing plugins for self-hosted WordPress sites.

- ◆ **Obox Mobile** (http://www. obox-design.com/wpmobile. cfm)—Create a custom experience for mobile users. Premium plugin priced at $60.

- ◆ **WordPress Mobile Pack** (http://wordpress.org/extend/ plugins/wordpress-mobile-pack)— Make your site accessible to mobile visitors with a mobile switcher, optional mobile themes, and widgets.

- ◆ **WP Mobile Detector** (http://wordpress.org/extend/plugins/ wp-mobile-detector)—Detect whether a site visitor is using a mobile device and, if so, switch to a WordPress mobile theme.

- ◆ **WP-to-iPad** (http://wordpress.org/extend/plugins/wp-to-ipad)—Optimize your WordPress site for iPad users.

- ◆ **WPtouch** (http://wordpress.org/extend/plugins/wptouch)—Transform your WordPress site into a mobile application, accessible by a variety of mobile devices including the iPhone, iPod Touch, Palm Pre/Pixi, BlackBerry, and Android devices.

IMPORTANT *Be sure to test your website on several mobile devices after installing a mobile plugin. Some plugins aren't compatible or effective with every theme.*

WPtouch offers a variety of options

Index